THE COMPLETE PUBLIC SPEAKER'S MANUAL

Covering every aspect of speechmaking, this guide will work
wonders for anyone — in any field of endeavour — who
wants to speak with the utmost ease and effectiveness.

GW00690791

THE COMPLETE
PUBLIC SPEAKER'S MANUAL
How to Get and Keep Control of an Audience

by

A.L.Kirkpatrick

THORSONS PUBLISHING GROUP

Wellingborough · New York

First published in the United Kingdom 1983
This edition first published 1986

Original American edition published by
Parker Publishing Company, Inc., West Nyack, New York, USA.

© PARKER PUBLISHING COMPANY, INC. 1981

British Library Cataloguing in Publication Data

Kirkpatrick, A. L.
  [Complete speaker's and toastmaster's desk
  book]. The complete public speaker's manual:
  how to get and keep control of an audience.
  1. Public speaking
  I. [Complete speaker's and toastmaster's
  desk book]   II. Title
  808.5'1   PN4121

  ISBN 0-7225-1373-9

Printed and bound in Great Britain

Dedication

To my good friend and fellow spokesman, Bob Hannegan.

How This Book Will Benefit You

Meetings! Meetings! Meetings! There are 100,000 meetings daily across America, according to the International Speakers Network. Where there are meetings, there are speakers—speakers of all kinds with varying degrees of speaking experience. Some are good, some are fair, but far too many are poor.

This difference in speakers, especially in their ability to deliver, can be readily observed during the proceedings of any convention program, whether it be a one-day meeting or a full week. Speaker after speaker is introduced to the audience as the program unfolds. You will see people glance at their schedule of events as one speaker finishes, then quickly leave the room before the actual introduction of the next speaker. You see, in a trade or industrial type of program, word gets around as to which speakers are worth hearing . . . and which are dull and boring.

You may also see members of the audience listen for a few sentences to a new speaker and then get up and leave. These are called *walk outs*. Do you have walk outs? If you lose just one member of your audience in this way, that's one too many. In this book you will discover how to correct that problem if you have it, and make all of your audience ready to hear everything you have to say.

You may also observe conventioners outside the meeting room during proceedings checking their programs and their watches. These people already know who they do not want to miss. You will see them move quickly into the meeting room when one speaker finishes, in time to hear the speaker they want to hear being introduced. Do you enjoy this type of speaking reputation?

Just remember that you are wasting your time, and more importantly, your audience's time, if you do not deliver well enough to get your message heard and understood.

It could be a civic club program. If you are a good speaker the audience probably already knows it and the club will enjoy record-breaking attendance. On the other hand, if you are a poor or mediocre speaker, they will know that too. Some will actually have their meal, lunch or dinner, make sure that they are marked present for attendance records, then leave before the program begins. If they don't know in advance, some of them may very well walk out after you get started. This applies to any type of one-speaker audience. There isn't much gray area. You can either deliver forcefully or you cannot.

There are no captive audiences. The speaker may captivate the audience but only with a sparkling delivery.

How do you stack up? You know the answer to that. In fact, you know better than anyone else. This book imparts the skills you need for a greatly improved performance on your very next appearance.

Do you have doubts? Do you sometimes wonder if you have the attention you would like to have as you deliver? This book will help you erase that doubt as you discover, among other things, the power of audience control.

Do you have trouble gaining control of your audience when you begin your speech? Do you sometimes appear to lose control as you move from point to point in your speech? Now you will find out how to gain control in a matter of seconds as you begin your speech, and you will learn how to maintain that control as you use the techniques suggested in this book. Improvement will be made in your very next talk.

Do you feel that humor in speaking is not for you? This book reveals how and when to apply humor. Once you gain this skill, it will help you get control quickly and keep it during your entire speech.

I became a student of speech making long before I decided to become a speaker. Because of this interest in effective speaking I was always in attendance at all speaking sessions, whether at a convention or the one-speaker type programs.

Early on I learned that those speakers who had mastered the use of humor, even if only sparingly, and could deliver a meaningful message with some degree of eloquence, were the same speakers who filled all of the seats and often spoke to SRO (standing room only) audiences. I began to study their styles and skills, being careful not to try to imitate. For more than ten years I spoke as a trade relations or industry relations speaker. Even now, as a professional, I continue to observe other speakers and the skills they use to win their audiences. You will discover these tried and true methods in this book. They work for the greats of the American Platform . . . they work for me . . . and these methods will work for you.

In addition to listening to and hearing from American Platform greats, I have also read just about every book on speaking that has been published. I continue to buy new books on speaking, and I have yet to read one that failed to help me become better at my craft of public speaking. Many speaker friends tell me that they do this too.

Today's audiences expect more and will not settle for a speaker who is not well prepared. They will not sit through a speech that has no sparkle and is not delivered forcefully. This book will help you accomplish both.

This book explains how to gain control quickly of your audience and to make speaking enjoyable and pleasant for you and, most importantly, more rewarding and satisfying for your audience. You will discover how to hold your audience so that all of your message is heard and appreciated. You will be invited back for return engagements before the same group for two reasons: one, you have a good message, and two, you deliver it with real impact. Your knowledge and ability to *control your audience* and share that knowledge will determine your success as a speaker. It is a great feeling.

From introduction to closing you will learn about delivery and audience control based on my 22 years as a speaker and speech trainer. Any speaker who reads and studies this book, using the techniques described, will become a better speaker immediately. You cannot fail to improve. Try . . . you must try. You must put this knowledge to use.

You will discover how to speak effectively as a panel moderator or as a panelist. You will learn how to serve as a roastmaster or as a roaster. You will improve your talent as a toastmaster or master of ceremonies.

This book will explain how to handle question and answer sessions, and how to prepare and conduct effective seminars. A quick review of this book from time to time will get you ready for any occasion so you can approach that actual speaking engagement with total confidence. Why? Because this book conveys every possible speaking assignment . . . even the eulogy.

This book will make your speeches a joy to deliver and a joy for the audience to hear. You will be invited back for repeat engagements again and again because you have something to say—and you say it well.

"Kirk" Kirkpatrick

ACKNOWLEDGMENT

My thanks to W. E. "Doc" Dimmock, who gave me my first assignment as an industry speaker, for his continued friendship and encouragement.

A.L.K.

Table of Contents

*****

1

How to Get
Audience Control
in Seconds

And now, it is a pleasure to present . . .

The time has come for you. The moment of truth. The point of no return. The program has moved along well; you learned more about the group in the last few minutes; you actually feel closer; the introducer has given the audience the pertinent facts about you, your qualifications, and their reasons for having you on the program with your subject. Now it is time for you to deliver.

This is the important moment—your first moment before the group. Some say this is the most crucial moment of your entire appearance. You are apprehensive and you should be. These next few moments will help in a big way to make your speech a success . . . or failure.

If your talk goes well, you will be on cloud nine. If it fails, you will feel defeated. If it doesn't go well, those 30 minutes up front will be an eternity.

You're on! Rise from your chair. Don't push yourself up with your arms as if it were a chore to rise to the occasion. Do it normally and do it with ease. You should be getting ready to rise as you hear the last few words of your introduction. Remember, all eyes are on you . . . and the judging has begun.

Move to Podium

Walk directly to the podium. Do not rush. Do not saunter. This is a dignified moment and you should act and look the part of the most important person in the room at this time . . . because for the next few minutes, that's your role.

Pause

Many speakers take a long pause just as they get to the podium. If you do this, be sure you don't stare at one or two people but instead let your eyes begin to move over the audience. The pause must not be too long. It should be brief and should convey to the audience that you are looking them over, getting a fix on their seating arrangements, and analyzing to get your proper range. It should also indicate that you intend to deliver a message to all of them. This pause should indicate that you are in complete command of the situation and you are merely getting ready to deliver. As you take this pause, breathe deeply, though not in a way that you appear to be nervous or out of breath. Just catch your breath as you pause.

Start Slow

Do not hurry. Take your time. Inexperienced speakers feel compelled at times to start talking the moment they get behind the microphone. This shows nerves. It could telegraph to the audience that you are not quite sure of yourself and that your nerves are about to get the best of you. This tends to make the audience uneasy, and there is no good reason why they should be uneasy . . . your apprehension is quite enough. If you plan to control your audience, you must show control yourself.

Thank Introducer

Thank the introducer, although that does not have to be the first thing you utter. Here is where you can pull some jokes on yourself that help to pull you down and humanize you. Two or three quips of one-liners will work wonders for you. You can easily use two or three quips as you first look at the audience from behind the mike. It helps your timing and pulls them together. In short . . . it helps the audience *accept* you . . . your first step to audience control. Your stories can be about good or bad introductions you've had before. You could say, "Unlike this good introduction I was just given, etc."

Your First Words

It is important to remember that often your best quips can come from something that actually happened during the meeting. However, most quips at this point are about speech making and are almost always premanufactured or "borrowed." Practice before using. A word of warning— never use quips that "put down" the introducer.

The introduction means a great deal to you. You are more likely to be overintroduced than underintroduced and audiences recognize this. Your ability to take it in stride wins points with your audience and from here on you want as many as you can get.

These quips, comments, or one-liners suggested for use just after your introduction are suitable for most any type of meeting where you are introduced as a featured speaker. This method is especially recommended for a breakfast, key-note, luncheon, or after-dinner engagement. Effective quips are important here because they help you get timing as well as analyze the audience response. Audience control cannot begin until you establish this rapport.

When Overintroduced

First, let's ask the question, "What can you do when you have been overintroduced?" The first rule is to use some lines that humble you, that pull you back down from the pedestal you have been placed on by the introducer. This will happen often because the program planners want the audience to feel that they have arranged an excellent program of important speakers. Here are some lines that will help you to let the audience know that you realize you are not quite that great. You should glance at the introducer and say to the audience:

I wish my mother could have heard that . . . she would believe it.

That was really good . . . sounded a little perfumy, but I learned long ago that a little perfume won't hurt you if you don't swallow it, and I'll try not to swallow it.

You should not use more than two of these lines at any one time in this way. Then go on to say, "Thanks for a really good introduction. I knew I was in good hands when we met (or when I learned that you would be the one to introduce me)." At this point, you turn to the chairman or president or the person presiding and say, "Mr. Chairman. . . ." (This is the first of several transition points in your talk.)

Many speakers leave off the "Mr. Chairman, Mr. President, Distinguished Guests, Ladies, and Gentlemen" and go right into their remarks. Sometimes, I like to acknowledge the leadership represented, but there is nothing sacred about this. It depends on how you view the occasion and how it fits your style. I usually save my acknowledgments for after "Mr. President," rather than immediately after the introduction.

Here are some more examples of one-liners or short

remarks you could make. These could be substituted for those just mentioned to give you variety. Remember . . . these are for after you have been somewhat overintroduced. Be sure to practice one-liners and short remarks. The importance of audience control lies not in what you say, but how you say it.

When you hear a speaker getting into this part of the talk in a tentative way, it is probably because not enough thought has been given to the quips and one-liners that are being used. I always make it a practice to review my quips and one-liners carefully . . . even out loud if time and circumstance permits. When you are tentative in your approach to the audience at this point, it takes you longer to gain control.

> The only thing wrong with that introduction is that it was exaggerated . . . but I liked it.

> I didn't expect that many good things to be said about me until they preached my funeral.

> That was a really fine introduction. Now I'm convinced that you people (looking at the audience) are fortunate to have me here to speak.

> That's the second best introduction I've ever had. The other day I was on a program like this and just before it was time for my introduction the person that was to introduce me became quite ill and I had to introduce myself. . . .

Here's another after-introduction comment that I've used with some success after having been overintroduced.

> That introduction is sort of like the little old lady who was downtown shopping and saw a dress in a store window where she didn't have a charge account. She liked it and went into the store, found the dress, took it over to the salesperson and said, "I'd sure like to have this dress. It's the last one in my size and I'm afraid it will be sold, but I don't

have an account with this store. Will you take my
personal check?"

"Yes, certainly," replied the salesperson, "if
you can identify yourself." So, the little old lady
reached down in her purse and pulled out her little
pocket mirror. After studying it a minute, she re-
plied, "Yes, it's me all right."

So, when I'm introduced that well and so many wonderful things are said, I like to double-check and be sure the
introducer is talking about me!

After Moderate Introduction

A moderate introduction is most desirable. It is not so
exaggerated that it is impossible to live up to the remarks
make by the introducer. Neither is it so low key that the
necessary credentials you bring to the occasion are not mentioned.

Here are some quips after a moderate introduction:

You forgot to tell them that I am a Notary
Public.

You left out the fact that I was an Eagle Scout.

The other day at a luncheon, they got ready for
me and the introducer said to the audience, "And
now it's time to introduce our gust of honor."

(If you use this one, be sure to enunciate the word gust
because it really doesn't sound that different from the way
some people might say guest of honor. If you are to get a
laugh from it, you've got to be sure they understand the word
gust.)

We get all kinds of introductions. In getting me
on the other day the introducer said, "I'm not going
to bore you with a long speech, but I'll introduce a
speaker who will."

(This almost always goes over because audi-

ences have all heard introducers do a poor job of introduction. They've all heard introducers become so nervous as they make introductions that they really do say the wrong thing, unintentionally, because of nerves.)

Never forget how important these first few moments are as you get started into your speech. The audience is already judging you and deciding whether you will be interesting or boring. Make everything count in your favor and you will have no problem gaining control.

Chuckles

The following remarks are not meant for anything more than chuckles. Seldom will you hear any real belly laughs at this point in a speech. Remember, these serve a purpose, that of giving you some remarks to let your audience know you do not take yourself too seriously.

There are occasions where it might be well to leave off quips that are meant for laughter. If you've been alert during the proceedings up to this point, you, as an experienced speaker, will have a good indication of what is in good taste and fits in properly . . . but always be watching for incidents that you can turn into a humorous remark. There are far more opportunities than you realize. Be alert to the possibilities, if you like this style of getting started.

Tested Openers

These openers are not new. Possibly you've heard some of them; they are still being used. In fact, I've used them recently with favorable results. You won't make your speech a roaring success at this point, but you can get your timing right and get into your speech in a satisfactory manner.

This is doing several things for you. It's doing the job of pulling you back down to earth, letting you show some humility, and letting the audience realize that while you're proud of your introduction and your credentials, you realize that your introduction did sound a little too flowery.

Loosen the Audience

Getting an audience to chuckle helps to loosen them up. If they'll laugh together, they'll listen together, and that is why a speech is made. An audience seems to feel that if a speaker opens with a few chuckles he or she won't be too hard to take. They're going to be able to enjoy the speech and they feel it's not going to be a blockbuster, fire 'n brimstone type of message in which they will have no lighter moments to relax.

You Relax, Too

An important consideration in using quips just after being introduced is that you are at the top of your speech. It gives you an opportunity to look around and make eye contact, to get to know the audience, to judge their ability to grasp what you're saying. Let's face it—some audiences are faster than others. When you use humor at the top, you have the opportunity to study how quick their reactions are likely to be to your remarks.

One more very important point . . . these lighter moments give you an opportunity to relax a bit more. The sooner you relax, the sooner the audience relaxes . . . and the time for control begins.

Speak Clearly

You must be careful to enunciate clearly in using humor, particularly here in the first part of your speech, because the audience is probably hearing you for the first time. To some extent, the listeners have to get used to your sound, your accent (if you have one), your tone of voice. If they fail to hear any of your words clearly, it will be at the top of your speech. Later, as they adjust to the sound of your words, it becomes a little easier.

You have probably seen stage plays where you had a difficult time for the first few minutes of the first act hearing clearly the words from the stage. After a few moments, you hear a little better and you begin to pick up the lines a little more easily. Be aware of this danger as you begin your speech.

A Word of Warning

It is unwise to be too sure of what kind of introduction you're going to be given. Quite often you'll anticipate how the introducer will introduce you and when it isn't done just that way, it has a tendency to throw you off guard, to get you off to a shaky start. If you get off to a shaky start you will not get control. Get off to a good start and *the power of audience control* begins early in your talk and is easy to maintain as you move from point to point. It works like magic! If you anticipate and plan your remarks in acknowledging the introduction one way and it's done a different way, you must adjust quickly.

Some speakers like to *fix* their introductions, meaning that they want certain points made that will provide an opportunity for their quips. This is dangerous except for a veteran speaker who can switch lines quickly and in a way that it doesn't show. You can never be sure it will be done the way you want. When it goes wrong, you're in trouble.

Some speakers will have their introduction read word for word and before it's over you realize that you and the audience are a bit bored and glad to finally hear . . . "it is a pleasure. . . ."

After Mr. President, Etc.

You have finished your quips after the introduction. If these were carefully selected and rehearsed, chances are you are off to a good start. You will have pulled the audience together a bit more because they listened together and chuckled together. This is using skill . . . your skill. And it is the beginning of audience control . . . your audience control.

You should now turn to the president or program chairman, if you use that style, and clearly say, "Mr. President," "President Jones," or in some cases, "President Bill," depending on who that person is and how well you know him or her. It may or may not be the same person who introduced you. After Mr. President, there should be just one or two specifically named dignitaries, such as Your Honor, Mayor Q; Your Honor, Governor R; Your Honor, Senator S; Your Honor, Congressman T; or maybe even President of Lions International or Lions District Governor, etc.

Some of these people will be at the head table; others will be in the audience. Be sure to know who they are and where they are sitting, or don't try to make such acknowledgments. It's better to ignore them than to do this poorly. Here is another potential problem. If you make mistakes in names or titles of special people in the audience, others will notice it, causing you to lose their attention. You could begin to stumble here in your presentation and lose momentum and, therefore, control. Get this over with quickly. Do it clearly and with emphasis, but remember that the audience did not come to hear a "roll call."

More One-Liners

Now this next phase should be considered carefully, using more quips as a further warm-up. It may not be necessary. It may not fit your style. This is referred to as softening up the audience. Normally, you could say:

>   *It's good to be here with you today . . . as a matter of fact, have you ever heard a speaker say he didn't want to be where he is today?*

After saying "Ladies and Gentlemen," as in the case of a convention-type meeting, you could say:

Delegates at large . . . Delegates at large are those men here without their wives.

After saying, "Mr. President, it's good to be here, etc.," you could comment by saying, "I want to do well" (for whatever reason you want to give) and then say:

Of course, you can't always be sure how well you'll go over. When it's all over, a speaker can't be sure whether the applause was for a good speech . . . or because the speech was over. A few days ago, while walking down the hallway at a break, I overheard a member of the audience say to a friend of his, "That speaker couldn't have been worse." His partner replied by saying, "Oh, yes, he could . . . if he had a little more time, he could have been worse." Now I'm sure it was one of the other speakers he was talking about.

After getting a few laughs in this early part of a talk, a good quip would be:

You folks are great! It's good to know that I am not going to participate in something like the Nuremberg Trials . . . or testify to the Grand Jury . . . or speak to a Sonotone Convention.

You can use one of these or all three. If you use all three, (Trials, Jury and Sonotone), you put to use the "rule of three," which is a tried and true method of getting a laugh. This line also provides an excellent opportunity to praise the audience for being alert and responsive.

Every step must be taken to keep your audience alert. Audience control cannot be attained if the audience is not with you and is not in step with your speech. You keep them in step and alert by carefully chosen remarks as you begin the opening of your speech.

Plan Your Opening

All of the comments and/or quips that are used after the introduction and after "Mr. President" should be planned in advance. Needless to say, *all* quips should be rehearsed. Most speakers will jot down a selection of two or three fast remarks to use after each step, using the key word they need as a reminder for each. They will, however, continue to watch for something happening in the meeting procedures, or anything that is up-to-the-minute for comment. When something up-to-the-minute can be used, be sure that the audience is fully aware of it so that you can make your comments quickly without having to explain.

Never begin a long story when you first get up or even after you've addressed the chairman. Use short, quick lines first; then if you decide to use two or three, let the longer ones come after the short one-liners.

In the early part of your speech you must move along briskly with your planned short, quick lines, as you begin to get your listeners to move along with you. Well-chosen one-liners work wonders for you here because the audience has to be alert to catch the punch line. Longer stories call for more attention. If the story drags out a bit as you tell it you may fail to get the audience at this crucial point in your speech and never gain control. . . or, if not, you may be slow in getting control.

Experience teaches which remarks are best for each occasion. Some will fit any type meeting. It is important to plan your remarks, but never, never read anything you want to be amusing or funny. You must have complete eye contact with the audience when any type of humor is used. You simply cannot maintain this eye contact if you are reading instead of talking. A smile or other form of facial expression helps to put your funny lines over and it is difficult to breathe life into your words if you read to the audience.

Key Words for Quips

Key words serve as reminders of your chosen quips or stories. In this way, you can merely glance at the key word representing the line or lines you are about to use, which helps in keeping the pace you have established. A quick glance at the key word and the story begins with little, if any, loss of momentum.

Here are some examples of key words:

Mother is the key word for your reminder of the quip, "I wish my mother could have heard that . . . she'd believe it."

Perfume is the key word for your reminder of the quip, "That was real good . . . sounded a little perfumy, but I learned long ago that a little perfume won't hurt you if you don't swallow it . . . and I'll try not to swallow it."

Exaggerated is the key word for your reminder of the quip, "the only thing wrong with that introduction is that it was exaggerated . . . but I liked it."

Funeral is the key word for your reminder of the quip, "I didn't expect to hear that many good things said about me until my funeral."

Fortunate to have me might be best for your reminder of the quip, "That was a really fine introduction. Now I'm convinced that you people are indeed fortunate to have me here to speak."

Second or **2nd** could be your reminder of the quip, "That's the second best introduction I've ever had."

It's me could be your key word for the "little old lady story."

Notary public—the key word for that line.

Eagle Scout—the key word for that line.

Gust—for the "gust of honor" line.

Bore—for the "not going to bore you" line.

Let's consider that you might use more one-liners as further softening up exercises after "Mr. President." Here are the key words or phrases that serve as your reminders:

Speaker where he is today may be necessary to get you into the line, "It's good to be here today with you people . . . as a matter of fact, have you ever heard a speaker say that he didn't want to be where he is today?"

Delegates will get you into and serve as a reminder for the line, "Ladies and gentlemen and delegates at large . . . delegates at large being those men here today without their wives."

Applause is your reminder for the line, "Of course, you can never tell how well you'll go over. When it's all over, you're never quite sure the applause is because it was a good speech . . . or because it is over."

Worse should easily serve as your reminder for the "couldn't have been worse" line.

Nuremberg, grand jury, sonotone will remind you of this line after you've had some laughter.

You are not likely to use this many one-liners, but it is a start for you. It is easy to get new lines for openers if you are on the alert for them and appreciate how opening remarks can help you get off to a good start and gain early control of your audience. And audience control is your major objective.

When Audience Is Responsive

You may be speaking on a program following one or more excellent speakers who have done a fine job of getting the audience in a good, responsive mood. Be thankful. This can help you to get off to a good start. Experienced speakers often find that it's easier to follow a good speaker than it is to follow a poor one. They see that the audience has been conditioned to being responsive and ready for more. In this case, it may not be necessary to spend much time with one-liners and softening up. You could use one or two quickly and get right into your speech. (One-liners and humor will be covered in more detail in a later chapter.)

Relax Your Audience

If the program is running late or behind schedule for one reason or another, as many programs do, you can help to relax your audience by saying that you're not going to keep them very long; you realize it's about time for lunch or you realize it's the end of a long day for them, or after dinner, and the hour is getting late. This says to the audience, "Look, I'm aware of this," and those who have never heard you before will not have to wonder if they're about to be subjected to a long, boring speech in which the speaker has absolutely no regard for their time. This is very important and is of real value in that type of situation. But do not let this sound as if you are apologizing. If all goes well and the meeting is on schedule, time and such matters should never be mentioned.

Butterfly Control

You've heard the old saying about butterflies in the stomach when you stand up to speak. The accomplished, effective speaker has learned to make the butterflies fly in formation. If you try to improve with each speech, stage fright ceases to be a problem and the butterflies are easy to handle.

The butterflies are in formation. You're off to a running start. The introduction went well. You acknowledged the introduction with sincerity, yet in a light-hearted manner. You let the audience know you are in control but that you don't take yourself too seriously. This is important. Too many speakers are pompous and it shows. No one likes that type.

Now you have relaxed your audience, and you, too, are

relaxed. Your eye contact has started; your timing is one step closer. All is well because you have gained control of your audience in the first few moments. Getting control of your audience does not just happen; it is planned. Professional speakers would never trust to luck in gaining control of an audience; careful planning is done, especially for those first few moments of the speech.

Ross Hersey, "King of the Shaggy Dog Story," says, "I always use one of my best stories at the beginning, and when it clicks . . . I know I am on my way."

You're on! Now you have to produce! You're into your talk. . . .

*****

Can anything go wrong? Yes!

Establishing Control Before the Audience Arrives

Before you ever go on . . .

You are on the scene. You begin to meet officials and program planners for this particular occasion. Here is where you take charge of yourself and the circumstances. This means being confident . . . and letting it show! Strive from the very beginning to have something of an authoritative air about yourself, but never an air of superiority. If you have any doubt about your role in the program, don't let it show. There is no reason for *everyone* to be worried.

Check Introduction

Learn who will introduce you and give that person your prepared biographical sketch, which provides facts for a meaningful introduction. You may have sent this bio in advance, but you should still check with the person who will introduce you. Be sure he or she has it and is prepared to give you a proper introduction. I always have an extra copy of my bio. You might say something like this, "Do you have what you need for my introduction?" If the answer is yes, then you could suggest, "Use as little or as much of my bio as you think necessary."

All too often, the introducer is inexperienced at introducing speakers. If you give instructions as to how you want to be introduced, it may unnerve that person and you will be improperly introduced. Be sure you have an easy bio to follow, and trust that it will be done well.

Conserve Energy

Don't knock yourself out trying to meet everyone in the group. This has a tendency to tire you and you'll need that stamina later. In the case of an evening meeting, be careful at cocktail parties. You can get into a meaningless conversation with someone who may destroy your mood for a good talk. Try to meet the principals and remember their names and titles, but don't try to show off your memory skills. It taxes your mental powers. Save your energy. Audience control is demanding—you don't want to tire out.

Following Other Speakers

If you are on a program behind another speaker or speakers, by all means sit in the audience and hear how it's going. You can study their timing and the audience's response. If it's going well, chances are you will too. If they are having trouble, you may spot the trouble and possibly avoid the same mishap. Begin to think what it will take to get the attention of your audience early in your speech in order to gain control.

If there is a scheduled lineup of speakers, which is common with convention-type programs, many experts suggest that you hear two or three speakers before you go on. You don't always have that much time and there is a danger to this approach: you can "lose your edge" as you wait to take part in the program. All of these things have a bearing on how it will turn out for you. The important fact is to be aware that your chances for success may begin *before* you even step to the podium.

Get Adjusted

If you still become nervous, a little apprehensive, maybe have a little stage fright, get to the meeting room or auditorium a little early. Look the room over. Get adjusted. Become familiar with that room. Whatever you do, go to that meeting room at least a few moments before you are to appear, so that you will have some feeling of familiarity with your surroundings.

Alan Cimberg, CPAE, the little man with a big message, from Malverne, New York, makes it a point to get in the meeting room several hours before he speaks so that he has a "feel" for his surroundings. Then he begins to think of how his presentation will be affected by room size, seating, acoustics and any other conditions that may have a bearing on the success of his program. It pays off for him; Alan Cimberg has been rated at the top for a number of years as a speaker. Most of his audiences are mass audiences and he will not trust to luck when it comes to that all important factor . . . preparation.

Think Positively

Have a talk with yourself. Yes, even brag on yourself a little bit. Lay it on thick. Get yourself feeling pretty good about you and your message, and it'll go a long way toward psyching you up and getting you ready. Tell yourself you look good, that you look successful. You want to look and feel good when you're facing that audience. Doing this mental exercise will help.

You do have to build your confidence occasionally, and when you psyche yourself up, you're in position to psyche up your audience. This is one way of saying you get their attention and get them to think your way. This is your objective, so get everything ready for a winner. There is no other way to think!

Take a tip from Dr. David Schwartz' best seller, *The Magic of Thinking Big*. Over and over he tells the reader, *Think Big! Think Big!* Point after point is made to prove that no one should ever sell themselves short. Dr. Schwartz is also a great platform speaker and he drives home these points over and over in his speaking appearances. Any speaker who will get ready for a meeting using these tried and true concepts of thinking big cannot fail to deliver enthusiastically. It's really quite simple . . . you feel good and positive about you and your message . . . and your audience will respond in a big way.

If arriving too early tends to bother you, then don't do it. Most speakers feel more comfortable about their upcoming speech when they have an opportunity to get into the room ahead of time. This way you can be sure there is nothing to distract you and therefore to detract from your presentation. Control your surroundings. Control your audience.

Set the Stage

All speakers have experienced incidents that had a decidedly adverse effect on the outcome of their talk, and hurt their overall performance. Don't make excuses . . . make good. Remember that you're there to win over an audience, not to place blame.

What about the meeting room? What about the facilities? What about the seating arrangement? Is it your concern? It should be if you want a winning performance.

Check Facilities

What can be done about these factors? The answer is simple. You get to the meeting room and check these important side effects that have such a bearing on your success.

If you are the only speaker, it's a bit easier to have the meeting room as you would like it. You can go to the meeting room well ahead of your actual speaking time and carefully check the arrangements so they fit your type of program. This is an important part of your getting ready for success. Leave nothing to chance.

Review Your File

You should have good information in your files on each particular engagement. Review it. Never let yourself get in the habit of speaking without reviewing your files. You are about to take part in a speaking program that will turn out to be a success for you . . . or be an embarrassing situation. Being ready with your message simply is not enough, and if you think it is, you are leaving out an important step—setting the stage with your own performance in mind. As a professional speaker, you want everything to work to your advantage. But it's up to you to see that it does.

Room Setup

If you are participating in a seminar, you will probably use props and will need to set up the meeting room differently than for a straight talk or lecture-type program. Review your purpose and make plans to see that you are set up properly. A small matter? No! It is vital to your success.

Audience Size

What size will your audience be? This is usually given to you in your correspondence prior to the meeting, . . . and usually it is exaggerated. Somehow program planners have a tendency to think big when they tell a speaker the size of his or her audience. At any rate, you should know the size before the meeting begins. You can find out by merely asking the program planner about the attendance . . how many can you expect in your meeting?

At this point your preparations should have you excited. You begin to feel you are ready and want your part to come soon. This is a good feeling and a sign that you are going to enjoy a good speaking experience. Let your excitement continue to build. Keep thinking of what a winning experience you are about to have. This enthusiasm will come through for you as you begin your speech . . . and help you to gain quick control.

Oversized Room

It is a good idea to take a quick count of the seats available for your session. Seating is highly important. Sometimes your alertness may lead you to make suggestions before the meeting gets underway. If there are too many seats available, then you know you will be speaking in an oversized room, which is one of the worst conditions you will ever have to face.

When a room is too large, the audience has a tendency to spread out over too large an area of the seating capacity. It is far more difficult for you to pull your audience together mentally if they are spread out physically over a larger area.

Whenever possible, get one of the program authorities to direct your audience down front, if necessary. When the audience is too far back it is much more difficult to establish a good rapport—to get their complete attention—to get audience control.

Good meeting planners do this automatically when they realize the room is too large. If they don't do this on their own, then suggest it. It is not good for the speaker to get introduced and then insist that those in the back rows come down front. Seldom does it come off well. If the seating isn't right when you are introduced, be prepared to face a tougher test in speaking.

If the number of seats are less than the size expected,

this too should be corrected, but it does not present the problem that an oversized room presents. The ideal is just the right amount of seats for your audience, but that's easier said than done. Do all you can to correct this situation.

Lectern

Examine the lectern. Are you familiar with the type? Some are different. You'll have a chance to learn more about this when the program gets started and others use it in the early part of the meeting. There will be times when all that precedes you will be your introduction. That is not enough time for you to check it. Ask for any adjustments you think are needed.

PA System

Checking the PA system is most important. You may be using a neck mike of some sort, such as those used with seminars when visuals are a part of the presentation. See that it has been delivered to the room. Leave nothing to luck. Get it and try it. Remember, from the time you hear, "It's a pleasure to present," you want to go for a winner. Make every detail work for you.

It may be that a change is needed for your presentation after the speaker ahead of you has finished. Careful attention to detail can help you to make adjustments quickly and without problems, thereby doing the audience a favor by not keeping them waiting. Don't take a chance on losing the audience's attention. It can be difficult to regain, so why gamble?

Easels

Do you need easels? Some speakers bring their own. If you need anything at all in the way of easels, have them brought into the room in advance. Study the best location for them. Check from the back and corners to be sure that your visuals can be seen easily. If you bring something to show, be sure that all can see it. These details are up to you and no one else.

Pointer

When easels are used it is good to have a pointer. The best answer to this is to have your own. I use a pointer that fits into my pocket like a ball-point pen. This is one worry I can forget when conducting workshops. Ask for the type you like to use as you check your needs.

Audio Visual

What about audio visual equipment? You need to spell out your requirements early in your negotiations with the program planner but there is still a big danger of it not being on hand when you are ready. This need should be at the very top of your list. Give it top priority or you will be racing around at meeting time looking for this equipment. Take care of this detail yourself as soon as you get there.

The better meeting planners ask for your requirements in advance when your date is confirmed. Even then, you should double-check to be sure everything is on hand before time.

Quite often projectors and equipment have to be rented for the occasion. This of course adds one more opportunity for a mix-up. Keep in mind that this type of equipment comes in various sizes, and speakers often feel that no two are exactly alike. Be sure to check it out carefully for your needs. It is imperative that you actually have a trial run with your materials so that you don't lose control after your meeting gets underway. . . or you will get off to a poor start and have a difficult time gaining control.

Once I was attending a civic club luncheon in which a projector was needed. No one, and this includes the speaker, took the trouble to be sure that this matter was taken care of in advance. The program had to start without it. They luckily found one in the building. Then the program had to be stopped so the projector could be hooked up. It was irritating to all in attendance, and what could have been a very valuable presentation turned out to be a poor program.

All too often these details are overlooked and failure is certain to follow. Usually a person who uses a projector needs it to make his or her program meaningful. Carefully check the details! It is the speaker who gets the blame, even if it was the meeting planner who was not prepared.

Trial Run

It isn't enough to have everything on hand—it must be checked out carefully. If using a film, put it in the machine and run it. If it is an overhead, check it out with your visuals. If part of your program calls for an audio-only presentation, see that your needs are in the room and see that they are in proper working order. Do not, I repeat, do not trust this assignment to anyone. Remember, *Murphy's Law* will take effect all too often, "anything that can happen, will happen." Never forget this. Hardly anything irritates an audience more than waiting for props to be put in working order.

Extension Cords

Your props often need extension cords to reach electrical outlets. Speakers who use these props often take along their own extension cords just to be safe. Put this on your checklist for getting ready.

Water

How long are you on? If it is a rather long workshop-seminar meeting you may want a glass of water close at hand. Generally, drinking water during a speech is not good practice, but it can be done without distraction as you get your audience involved. If you think you might need a bit of water to help your throat as you work, by all means have it close at hand and easy to sip from without annoying your audience. Don't use ice water; room temperature water is more relaxing to your throat.

Chalkboard

Is a chalkboard necessary for your presentation? If so, be sure it is in the room. Place it for your best advantage. Be sure you place it so everyone can see. All too often, chalkboards are placed in the meeting room without chalk or eraser. You can place the blame, but it will not improve your speaking skills or help you deliver a winning message.

There is no one connected with your meeting who will be as concerned as you about its success. If you are to maintain audience control, double-check everything. Then double-check it again.

Air Conditioning

Some meeting rooms have noisy air conditioning that can cause you problems. See if it can be adjusted quickly. Maybe the building engineer can find a way to cut down on the noise if it cannot be totally eliminated.

Temperature

If a meeting room or auditorium is warm before the audience comes in, it will very likely be too hot when it is filled with people. It can also be too cold for comfort. It is important to do what you can to arrange as much comfort as possible for your audience. Getting into the room before your program offers an opportunity to set things right. Do all you can to improve meeting conditions. It will pay big dividends in the long run. Most importantly, you may be able to remove some of the pitfalls to a successful performance.

Lighting

It is highly important that you see your audience as you deliver. You need to be able to see their faces—to see the reaction in their eyes. Eye contact, as you speak, cannot be overstressed. If the audience is in the dark or in a darkened room, you lose this valuable aid in helping you to get control. Nothing plays a more important part in holding attention than your ability to establish eye contact. It cannot be done in a darkened room.

If part of your program calls for visuals that look better in a darkened room, then be sure you get the lights back up as soon as you go into the lecture part of your presentation.

Maybe something ahead of you on the program calls for a darkened room. If so, get the lights back up for your talk. Many speakers avoid visuals for that reason. You may need to insist on better lighting, so do it. You suffer more than anyone if your part doesn't go well.

Jim Wolfe, Vice President of Welch Foods, in a variety of annual meetings, uses every conceivable type of audio and visual equipment, in addition to handouts and promotional items. He still insists on personally checking out the equipment and all material to be used. His meetings are consistently successful.

Handouts

Seminar and various types of workshop meetings often call for handouts. This applies particularly to professional training meetings, such as sales and management-type seminars. The handouts then become a part of your props, and you must plan carefully for them.

Being sure you have enough to go around is of primary

importance. To be safe, take along a number of extra copies of each piece. It is far better to have some pieces left over than to run short and leave part of your group without copies and having to look on with someone else. If the handouts are going to be included in a three-ring binder, have the holes punched in advance.

If you have to use a number of pieces as handouts, you may want to distribute them all at once just before the meeting gets underway. Distribute handouts for your full session if there is no break. If there is a break or more than one break, hand out only the amount needed to get to the break. This is difficult to time and plan, but you will be much better off than if you are constantly stopping the proceedings in order to distribute more materials. If your meeting moves along well, there is only a small danger that those in attendance will read on ahead of you.

The skilled seminar leader spends a great deal of time carefully planning how and when his or her materials will be distributed. Too often, meetings get off the track if this part is handled poorly. Get it all planned in advance. If your material is worth giving out, it is worth your attention to do it properly.

Time Allotment

Review again your time allotment. Your letter of invitation will usually include this information. If not, the actual program bulletin or final program will make it clear. On the day of the meeting, double-check this detail with the program planners. This can help as you get yourself ready. It also helps as you ready your materials and plan your opening remarks.

Audience Analysis

When you see your audience for the first time, or as they come in, mentally review what you know from advance notes. If this is a one-session occasion, all of these check-points become more of a must. You're getting everything ready to put your best foot forward. Don't let a few last-minute details seem unimportant. Age, occupation, and primary interests should be reviewed as you look them over.

Now you are ready. You've done all you can do to ensure success on this particular occasion—except the actual delivery. . . .

*****

Back to the speech!

Secrets of Maintaining Audience Control and Interest

Give it the light touch . . .

> *"As I was leaving the hotel this morning, a doorman asked me, 'Where are you bound for, General?' When I replied, 'West Point,' he remarked, 'Beautiful place, have you ever been there before?' "*

The above paragraph was the first spoken by General Douglas MacArthur in his farewell speech to the cadets at West Point. This speech entitled, *Duty, Honor and Country*, was also an acceptance speech for the coveted Sylvanus Thayer Award for service to the nation. He had no prepared text, not even notes.

No doubt all who heard him that day knew that his permanent residence after his retirement from the Army was the Waldorf-Astoria Hotel in New York City. All who heard him knew that for a period of time in his career he was the top ranking officer at West Point. The General used this opening as a touch of humor. It also helped to humanize him a bit in the minds of his audience, the cadets at West Point.

General MacArthur was a very accomplished speaker. He used these opening lines as a means of getting his timing as well as a means to establish eye contact and to prepare to deliver a memorable speech that was recorded and reprinted as a remembrance of his last trip to West Point.

If a person, as famous and as revered by his audience as General MacArthur, felt the need to use a definite speech technique to command attention and secure control, then all who make speeches should be guided accordingly.

Let's examine the opening remarks of another world-famous speaker to see how he uses the light touch in getting into a banquet speech. Neither used quips after their introduction but merely as they took command at the podium.

This is how Ronald Reagan responded to his introduction at the 28th Annual Sausagia Dinner in Atlanta at the Peachtree Plaza Hotel. He was the principal speaker and followed several preliminary speakers.

> "Thank you very much. Thank you, Mr. Toastmaster. I am glad there was a pause between the Battle Hymn of the Republic and getting me up here because I had just suddenly swallowed a baseball. You have honored me. I'll tell you . . . after all we have heard tonight . . . the humor I have heard from this platform, the wonderful music . . . I feel about as necessary and important as a young college student in a small town when a stranger in town asked one of the old-timers, 'Isn't there anything to do in this town? Isn't there a movie theater, or something to do for entertainment?' and the old-timer said, 'No, but we've got a freshman home from college, come on in the drugstore and look at him.' "

Many feel that Ronald Reagan is one of the best platform speakers in America today. If he feels the need to warm up his audience with levity before getting into his main subject, then it must be good advice for all of us who want to get better.

In this particular speech he came right back again with more humor, possibly because it was a banquet and he felt the need for more warm up.

> *"Now, we all have a lot of troubles and problems. Not too long ago out in Las Vegas, I addressed a convention of the American Cattlemen's Association. On the way in, a fellow recognized me and said, 'What are you doing here?' I told him that I was going to speak to the Cattlemen's Association, and he said, 'What's a bunch of cattle farmers doing in Las Vegas?' And I said, 'Buster, they're in an occupation that makes a Las Vegas crap table look like a guaranteed annual income.' "*

And once again, Mr. Reagan used the light touch to get himself and his audience ready for a more serious message when he remarked:

> *"I have a friend who is a businessman and every day on his way to work he has to go past a mental hospital. Every day he stops his car there because out on the grounds there is an inmate (a patient there) who is pitching an imaginary ball game. He stands there, gets his sign from the imaginary catcher, goes into his wind up, and then pitches an imaginary ball. I finally asked him one day, 'Why do you stop every day and look at that poor fellow?' He replied, 'Because the way things are going, I'll be there soon and I'll probably be catching him and I want to see how his curve breaks.' "*

Plan in Advance

Planned material is excellent to use at the beginning. Anyone could take these lines and use them as effectively as Mr. Reagan did, and for the same purpose, which was, no doubt, planned in advance. It is a method for getting started.

It is an effective speaking skill that I recommend whole-heartedly.

These excerpts from speeches delivered by great speakers are used here to point out the humorous remark as a means for beginning your speech. In Chapter 1, examples were given somewhat like these to point the way to use humor immediately after the introduction. Both methods are good. You are apt to hear many professional speakers use humor at the beginning to get their timing, their eye contact, and to relax. These are keys to getting the audience's attention and gaining audience control.

Attention for Main Message

You must now get favorable attention for your main message. Extreme care must be taken to ensure that your next few sentences will get favorable attention. It's usually good to actually state your central theme, then give a preview of what you will cover. Be careful that you don't say too much or give them a summary. Your theme, in fact, your speech title, should be short and provocative, but not too revealing. Because of this your central statement should fit this formula.

Many speakers have their own causes to speak for and these speech techniques work just as well for them as they do for a famous speaker. It's a skill. It calls for planning and it gets results. You get control of your audience and as you continue to use speechmaking skills you keep that control.

State Startling Facts

State some hard facts. You may use some startling facts taken from the body of your speech to give you a forceful attention-getting opening. This is an opening with real impact. What you have just said—those startling, shocking facts—may be frightening facts, depending on your subject. If it's a talk about legislation against crime increase, then you start with some facts to get their attention.

It may be that you would start out with a shocking statement. You might ask a question to pique their curiosity. You could possibly start out with a human-interest story. Regardless of what you use, it must relate to your main message.

Some speakers frequently let one of their principal visuals get the attention. This may be used effectively if visuals are used at or near the beginning of the presentation.

TV and Motion Picture Technique

Think of the motion pictures you've seen in which some of the opening scenes are designed to grab your attention and hold it. TV uses this often. They want to keep you glued to that picture, to not turn the dial, so they give you something out of the ordinary, something that is a sure-fire attention-getting part of the story right at the front, even before the credits are given. Now it takes skill to do this as a speaker and a lot of things must be taken into consideration. It is a good technique but it calls for skill and rehearsal.

A few years ago in my earlier days as a speaker, I was speaking on a program in Columbus, Ohio right after a lunch. The audience had finished cocktails and a heavy lunch and were somewhat sluggish. I started my talk with some information taken from the middle of the speech as a method of getting their attention and it failed . . . it failed miserably. That audience needed a warm-up type of opening. Had I known then what I've since learned about how to start, how to begin, I probably would have used a few quips at the top hoping to get a few chuckles, maybe a belly laugh, and then settle down to the somewhat serious message that I was to deliver.

I don't recall that we had any walkouts on that program, but I never got their attention. I never had the audience with me from point to point in what had been a somewhat successful speech at other meetings of that type. Inexperience on my part caused me to use the wrong type of beginning and I never recovered during the remainder of the speech.

Time of day and circumstances do have an effect. The more you speak, the more you'll realize you must take all things into consideration.

Memorize Opening

Should your opening be memorized? Yes, it should. It is one of the most important parts of your speech. You can get attention quickly or you can fail to get it for quite awhile. There's always the danger that you'll talk for some time without getting the audience's attention. You can look out at that audience and almost see your statements bouncing off their foreheads. It may be well for you to have a specific kind of opening. Memorize it so there's no way to get off to a poor start. The beginning of your speech is the most important part of it. So give your introductory remarks with some snap and punch

Mixed Audiences

The early part of a talk may have to be changed a bit when both men and women are in attendance. This is particularly true when the organization is for men or women only and their spouses are with them, such as Ladies Night or other special events.

Often program planners ask for more humor because of nonmembers who are attending. They feel the nonmembers, while interested in the message, are not quite as intent, not quite as interested in the meeting theme, etc. Rest assured that the right choice of stories will go extremely well with both the men and women. A mixed audience laughs better.

Don't worry too much about risqué stories as long as they are not downright blue. Today's newspapers, magazines and, most of all, television, have preconditioned all types of audiences to risqué stories. As long as you don't get off-color, here are some good ones:

After saying that the wives always make a contribution to their husband's success, you could say,

> *Of course, there are exceptions. A friend of mine told me about being at the dedication of a great new hotel in Houston, Texas, the land of the "big" rich. He said he overheard a man say, "My wife made a millionaire out of me." This prompted my friend to ask, "Well, what were you before?" The Texan replied by saying . . . "I was a multi-millionaire."*

> *A few days ago I jokingly asked my wife, "What would you say if I told you I was going to get a Mexican divorce?" She quickly replied, "Ole."*

> *"My friends call me Rover . . . because I am in the doghouse so much."*

> *One fellow said that his wife could never be an after-dinner speaker . . . she can't wait that long.*

A speaker could say just as he begins his speech that he realizes his audience is quick and alert . . . and continue,

> *I find myself pretty much like the fellow whose wife caught him accidentally at the lingerie counter . . . what I say had better make sense.*

There will be more about mixed audience humor in the chapter on humor.

Outline

When you go to the podium, take along your manuscript, your 3 x 5 index cards with notes, or your printed key-word outline. An outline is all that you should try to memorize. This key-word outline is used by professionals and can be used only by those who know their subject inside out and have studied the material over and over.

Don't Hide Your Notes

Don't try to hide the fact that you are using a manuscript, note cards, or a printed outline. This will indicate to the audience that you are trying to put one over on them, and your credibility will be doubted. On the other hand, there is no reason to wave your notes, hold them up, or in some other way advertise the fact that you have some written material with you.

Know Your Material

Regardless of your method, know your material so well that you are quite familiar with its contents and its sequence. Too many people stand up to use a manuscript that was prepared by someone else. There is nothing wrong with that, provided you have read it, reread it, studied it and even penciled in special thoughts, etc., in the margin. This also applies to the use of 3 x 5 index cards.

Today's modern audiences do not expect an off the cuff, spirited talk from people who are not professional speakers. They do expect and, in fact, demand that that person, regardless of his or her position, knows the material so well that he or she can look up at the audience frequently. This can be done effectively with the manuscript, the cards, or the keyword outline.

There are speakers who speak often, and who feel it is important to use a manuscript. They are so skilled you can hardly tell they have a manuscript with them at the lectern. They look up at the audience as often as possible. They have learned to read the beginning of a sentence and then look at their audience for the rest of that sentence. Practice looking at your manuscript or notes with just a glance so you won't have your eyes glued to your paper when you should be looking at your audience.

Depending upon the occasion, you might want to use the modern teleprompter, which reflects the manuscript on a glass in front of you. These are used in large meetings such as the huge political conventions. The person who is skilled at it appears to be hardly reading the notes. If you do read, look up frequently and, by all means, give your message with feeling.

Getting Attention

Break into the audience's thoughts—capture their imagination, and their attention so that you can gain audience control at once. Here again, I'm talking about the first few minutes of your talk where the audience decides to tune you in . . . or tune you out. All too often, speakers get up and go on with a lot of dribble about how they got there and where they have been speaking—things that in no way help to get the attention of the audience, let alone hold their attention.

Additional One-Liners

Many accomplished speakers like to get the attention of the audience by a few more one-liners. Maybe your attention-getting statements did not capture their full attention. You must have their attention or you will never get control.

Why do you have to think in terms of getting an audience's interest? First of all, those people may have many other things on their minds . . . situations back at their offices or even family problems. They are sitting there waiting. If you don't have the skill as a speaker to get their attention and make them *want* to listen to you, then you are likely to fail. If you don't get their full attention, there can be no communication, and therefore, no control. When you have control of your audience you can get them to act on your recommendations. You must first get their attention and then gradually lead them where you want them to go in their thought and in their action. There is real power in speaking once you get control of the audience and skillfully lead them from point to point as you deliver your message.

Later, you must begin to fill your speech with high points. Use all the skills you can master to hold their attention once you have it. At this point, be concerned with getting *favorable* attention. Later, you will get into *holding* their attention.

Regardless of who you are, how popular or how powerful you are, how much charisma you have, no matter how important your message is, or how well-versed you are on that message, the actual "proof-of-the-pudding" is the delivery of that message to your audience. You cannot place too much emphasis on the delivery. Just as in selling, if you can't tell it . . . you can't sell it!

Lead In

Don't jump right into the middle of the speech. Lead into it, and it shouldn't take many sentences or a lot of time to do. Just set up the points that you are to cover: here it comes; pay close attention! I go by the belief that when you make a speech it is somewhat like a drama or a scenario for a play. You get the hero (audience) in trouble; then you get him (them) out.

Think of all the books you've read and all the dramas you've seen. They always get the hero *in* trouble, and then get him *out* of trouble, point after point after point. Give your points about why it's necessary for us as a group—you as a speaker, they as an audience—to spend time on this subject now.

You should not leave an audience without giving suggestions for solving whatever the problem is that you brought out in the first part of your speech. Neither should you leave an audience without clearly stating the action they should take. Be specific. Tell them how! Today! Call for action! Ask for the order!

A speaker acquaintance of mine recently prepared a new and special speech for an audience he wanted very much to impress. He did an excellent job in researching the problems he wanted to discuss. He had excerpts from articles and even short clippings on the subject taken from magazines and newspapers. For some 40 minutes he cited those problems for this group. He really gave a fire-and-brimstone message while covering the problems. Unfortunately, he did not have any time left for suggestions to solve those problems, nor was he forceful in his close. I was in that audience, and needless to say he left the audience depressed. Always, always, try to leave your audience on high. Tell how they can solve their problems.

I'm reminded of a program I did not too long ago. I was the fifth speaker in the morning. Each speaker seemed to get worse as far as the problems they were setting forth for the attention of this international convention. This was topped off by a Washington bureaucrat who dug their graves a little deeper.

As I sat there hearing those speakers, I could look out in the audience and see that they were getting gloomier and gloomier. So, rather than putting anything at the top of my talk that sounded or appeared to be a problem, I merely said something like, "Well, we do have problems. Our forefathers had problems. We'll always have problems. It'll be people like you and I who'll solve these problems and here's how we'll do it."

In less than 25 words, I went right into my suggested game plan, my suggested formula for continued success. In a sense, it was an easy spot for me to fill, because the audience was waiting for something constructive they could consider. They wanted something that they could feel would give them an opportunity to continue their success stories rather than something negative and frightening.

Rate of Speech

Rate of speech means how fast you should talk. You will find it extremely difficult to become a slow speaker or to slow down your speech if you are used to a fast delivery. If you are a slow speaker, you'll find it extremely difficult to speed up your speech, but there is a happy medium.

If you speak too slowly, you'll be guilty of droning on, and there's nothing more boring than this kind of speaker. If you speak too fast, you are going to chew up some words from time to time. Usually any word in any given sentence potentially can change the sentence, so be doubly careful.

Speech experts usually recommend somewhere in the range of 110 to 120 words per minute as satisfactory. You can practice with a stop watch as you rehearse or tape and then check the time. You must still adjust to each audience and you learn to do this by analyzing for improvement.

As you progress and speak more, you will develop a knack of getting in step with your audience's ability to receive your message. You will notice sometimes that you will be talking and it appears that nothing is going into their heads. This isn't likely to happen if it is slow, but if it is too slow, the audience will get tired of waiting for the next word. If it's too fast, you'll be constantly losing them. And this will show in their faces.

Every experienced speaker knows that his or her tempo will be to some extent dictated by the response of the audience, because there really is an audience "feel" that plays back to you and tells you how you're doing. Learn to improve your own speaking rate so you can establish a rate of speech suitable to each audience. The more you speak, the better you become in judging the proper speed.

Recently I helped a speaker who droned on and on; his pitch and speed were the same. They were beautiful words well said, but the speech had no excitement because his pitch never varied. After we worked on this monotone, his speeches improved rapidly and he has become an accomplished and very popular speaker, much in demand.

Be Understood

What do I mean by making yourself understood? The purpose of your speech is to either instruct, inform or entertain. Regardless of which one, if the audience doesn't understand what you're saying and the meaning you want to convey, then you are failing as a speaker. You must give your talks in simple language. Reread the Gettysburg Address; reread the Sermon on the Mount; analyze the most famous orations of all times; and you'll find that they are all in simple language. It's very important that you keep this uppermost in your mind. If they don't understand you, then you will fail to get and hold their attention.

Delivery

The nature of delivery depends on the occasion. A eulogy speech would certainly be a different type of delivery than a keynote speech or an after-dinner speech. Academic, yes, but you do need to rethink these thoughts at times.

Think in terms of body movement—how you move on the platform, how you move across the stage if you're handling certain things—all have a bearing on the reception of that audience. Don't make short, choppy, nervous, jerky gestures because they distract. You can overdo the gestures by putting too many in your delivery. Your voice . . . the loudness, the distinctiveness, the pitch, the timing, the intensity . . . all affect your total delivery.

The only way you can critique your full delivery is to have a video playback. This method is becoming increasingly popular.

The important point to make is "if it's worth doing, it's worth doing well." Delivery of your message is what this book is about, so that you can be classified as an effective speaker . . . not someone just filling a spot on the program.

I like the way Don Hutson, CPAE[1] and past president of NSA[2] emphasizes the importance of the speaker's audience. He says,

---

[1]CPAE is the most coveted award given by NSA. It is reserved for the very few who reach the highest level of professionalism, as determined by their peers.

[2]NSA is National Speakers Association, an organization of the best platform speakers in America. It also includes a growing number of speakers from abroad.

"A painter can paint alone, a writer can write alone, a composer can compose alone, but a speaker cannot speak alone. The more you understand your audience the better you can deliver your speech. There is a closeness between speaker and audience that is pleasant to experience when both understand that they need each other."

* * * * *

You're off and running!

4

How to Establish Immediate Rapport and Understanding

Be sure your speech fits the group . .

Speeches are made for one of three reasons: one, to *inform* only, such as a briefing-type appearance; two, to *motivate* a group to take some form of action on a given cause, as political candidates (possibly to inform and to motivate), or to inspire and motivate a sales force to greater sales results (here again a general sales meeting could be to inform of new products or new methods or new programs, yet still include material that will motivate them to action); three, to *entertain* only, such as the after-dinner type speech situation when the program people want to let their group off of the serious subjects and relax, such as a monthly or annual organization banquet.

Regardless of which of the type speeches mentioned above, always remember that the meeting is absolutely meaningless if the power of audience control is not put to use. Practically all of the speech skills already covered apply here with good judgment as to their application. The sales manager may think he or she has a captive audience when his or her sales force is put together. Not true! You may have captive bodies in a group but you don't deliver a speech to bodies. A speech is delivered to *minds*, and you must control those minds if the speech is to get the desired results . *action*.

Primarily I am talking here about the speech to inform, to brief, and to motivate. Humor will be covered in a later chapter and will deal primarily with the totally humorous-type talk. The speech explained now could include and probably should include something in the way of levity, but only as a tool for changing direction.

Previous chapters discussed the methods for first looking at the audience and acknowledging your introduction, while using quips and one-liners to secure immediate control of the audience. Chapter 1 discussed a method for using another quip or two, preferably one-liners, after addressing the chairman of the meeting or those who need to be addressed, in an attempt to get even better attention, better control and also help to humanize the speaker.

The second chapter told about how to be sure that the meeting room and facilities and all in connection with props and materials are checked carefully before meeting time to be sure that nothing goes wrong.

Chapter 3 dealt briefly with quips after the introduction or Mr. President, how to get into a couple of light short stories and move even further along into gaining control of the audience. This isn't always needed but it is practiced by the most skillful speakers.

Now let's talk about how to magnify your central theme. First and foremost, you must be absolutely sure of the audience you are addressing. This seems academic, but speakers can be wrong about their audience just as an audience can wrongly prejudge a speaker. Know the audience before you arrive and get your first look at them. Regardless of the type, age group, or profession of the audience, your remarks must be of interest to them, or they will not be listening. It is important that your preparation takes this into account.

One common denominator used by skillful speakers

that fits almost every audience, particularly management people, is to talk in terms of people problems and how to solve them.

Getting Your Range

During those first few moments of your acknowledgment, your recognition of the chairman and others, you should be making mental notes about the audience's attention and interest level. You can see if your audience appears to be hearing you throughout the room. For example, if you've used a one-liner and they laughed well down front but not in the rear, then it is possible that they did not hear you in the back of the room. It goes without saying that there isn't any use to making a speech if the entire audience doesn't hear what you're saying. So, here a little more time is provided for you to get a range, get a fix on how loud you're speaking and how well the PA system is picking up your remarks, and if you are indeed being heard throughout the entire meeting room or audience.

Speech Speed

As I have said, the rate of speaking satisfactorily to most audiences is from 110 words a minute to 120 words per minute. They can listen to this comfortably and carefully. It is seldom that an audience cannot hear and understand what you are saying at this rate of speech. Quite often there will be audiences that could take it in faster. Watch carefully to gauge the listening ability of your audience. See how well they appear to be listening. This will let you judge the speed at which you move along.

Pronunciation—Enunciation

As stated before, the early part of your speech is the most important. The audience needs to hear clearly what you have to say. This is vital to gaining control. Whatever you do speak carefully these first few moments as you spell out and magnify your theme to be sure the audience clearly understands what you are saying. This is another reason for moving along rather slowly for the first few minutes. You can do this by careful observation of the audience as you speak. As you gain in experience you'll be in a better position to evaluate their listening ability as it relates to pronunciation as well as speed of delivery. Be careful that you don't slur your words or "chew them up" and make them difficult to understand.

Talk to Listeners

Don't orate; use a pleasant and easy manner. Don't be afraid now and then to insert a short impromptu remark, probably something that has happened in the program. This gives it color. It also indicates to the audience that you are alert to where you are, who they are, what has been happening, and in general what has taken place in the program. All of these are added skills in helping you to reach a good rapport between you and your listeners, the audience.

The Manuscript

If this is a talk in which a full manuscript is used and you have practiced it carefully but still feel the need to have your manuscript at hand to read verbatim an important passage, let your manuscript rest on the podium. Learn to glance at it frequently for guidance but look mostly at your audience. If you read it word for word you will never get the attention of your audience. In other words, don't chain yourself to that manuscript because you are then guilty of delivering a "paper." Audiences do not like this type of delivery, if they expected a speech.

When you look at your audience, look at all of them. Keep your eyes slowly moving around as you look up from your script. Look in a different direction frequently. Whatever you do, don't let them feel that you are doing this in a mechanical way because eye contact is important. Certainly you must look at them long enough for them to feel that you really are looking at them rather than practicing a speech skill. As you get better and better with your delivery and with your material, it is amazing how often you can look up and still carry on exactly what you meant to say. Keep in mind that if you do not say it exactly like it was prepared, as the manuscript reads, no one will know it but you. There is no damage done from getting a word into the message that is slightly different from the prepared manuscript.

Using Gestures

Although a later chapter gives you more description of gestures, here is where you begin to let your hands and your arms and all of you get into the speech. Keep in mind you are getting ready to magnify your central theme, and without any feeling in it, it certainly will not appear that you are into your subject well enough to be taking up their time. It is important that you begin to loosen up right here because as you get further into your speech it becomes more automatic. You may need to think about gesturing in the early part of your speech more than you will later.

When you get all fired up and begin moving along at a faster pace with more feeling, gestures will come naturally.

Get to the Point

Too often we see speakers on a convention-type program who go too long with the humor and the small talk, and the audience begins to get a little restless. They wonder when they're going to hear the message they were told they were going to hear. Get into the main part of your speech as quickly as you can. This can be done in several ways as mentioned in the previous chapter; use an anecdote or a bit of humor, or maybe challenge them or ask a question. There are many ways in which this can be done.

Illustrate Your Ideas

Good anecdotes are very good for this part in the program. After all, you're still leading them along with you. You haven't gained the sufficient momentum to feel that you really have complete control. Your audience can be lost in the early part of the program if these practices of good delivery are not put to use.

Here is a practical example of how simple, graphic, straightforward language can help so much in getting attention. I tell the audience of an example of this type of communication. While going from the airport to a hotel in Orlando, Florida, the driver of the bus seemed to be quite enthused about his city and its growth. He began to tell us about the new buildings, new hotels, and general improvements that were being made. We passed one building site and he pointed out that a new building was going up there that would be one and a half times larger than another building that he pointed out to us. It happened to be another hotel. He could have used square feet, he could have used the number of stories high, he could have used many comparisons, but by simply saying that on that site a new hotel is going up that will be one and a half times larger than this one over here was usefully simple. This is a good method for demonstrating in the early part of the talk how simple language helps to get your point over.

Don't Orate

Most speakers merely make talks, speeches, or give presentations. Seldom is real oratory used any more. When you think of oratory you think of the Gettysburg Address or William Jennings Bryan's Cross of Gold speech. That is a type of speech most of us will probably never be called on to deliver. Just state the facts; tell the audience what you are there to talk about; and add to it living, breathing examples of what it means to them. Always keep in mind that if you cannot relate your subject to that audience, then you really have no business standing before them. Speaker after speaker gets up and begins to talk about something that is of no real interest to that particular audience.

Several years ago I attended a black tie banquet of a professional organization in which they were honoring their best performers. Something in the form of an Oscar was being given to the top winners and they had a guest speaker who was president of a sizeable university. Now of that audience there probably was not two percent who were graduates of that university or two percent who were even very interested in its fiscal programs. This speaker, from the time he acknowledged his introduction, began to review (believe it or not) his budget for the coming school year. Shortly after he started, and the audience began to see what he intended to discuss, you could look around the room and see that absolutely no one was interested. Some were even looking at each other as if to say, "what on earth are we doing here? What business do we have listening to this program at this time?" Needless to say, the speech was a total flop and the officers of the organization and program planners were severely criticized by their members for having put on the program a person whose academic credits were outstanding, but who did not take the time to prepare for this particular meeting. An extreme example but true, and one that is experienced too often in meetings.

Explain Why You Are There

Often the chairman or person who introduces you will qualify you as a speaker on a particular subject, but it is still up to you to create a relationship between you and the audience, your topic and that audience, and why you are qualified to discuss it. This is not meant to be rehashing the introduction but merely to say something like, "When I was invited to this occasion to discuss this subject, I was quite pleased to accept because it's something that I feel is important for all of us. I'd like to share my viewpoints on this particular subject with you." Then state your central idea. Tell it clearly and directly. This is really the foundation of your speech so be sure that your audience understands it.

The story is told about an old southern minister who seemed to have the rapt attention of his congregation every time he got in the pulpit to deliver a sermon. A visiting minister asked him one day after a particularly good sermon, "How on earth do you get such good attention? How is it that you have such a good turnout every Sunday, and deliver such a meaningful and interesting sermon? How do you prepare?" The old minister replied, "Well, it's a simple formula as far as delivering my sermon is concerned. I learned it from someone else and I'm certainly willing to share it with you." He went on, "First I tell 'em what I'm going to tell 'em, and then I tell 'em, and then I tell 'em what I told 'em." Now you see what he did was to follow a simple but basic rule of communication. He announced his subject, gave his subject, and then gave a brief recap of his subject.

Be careful in speaking that you do not summarize too quickly at the outset, when merely telling the audience what you are going to talk about is sufficient. There is an equal danger of making the review at the end too long. All that is necessary, as you will find out later, is to just recap the basic points that are covered.

I and You

It is so easy for a speaker to begin to use the personal pronoun "I" too much, to overwork it. It is good speaking practice to talk to the audience as *you*, to you people or to your organization. When you do this, of course, it puts that much more pressure on you to relate your subject to the audience. Keep this in mind not only in preparation but, even more importantly, keep it in mind as you begin to deliver, regardless of whether it's in manuscript form, an index card outline system, a roughed-out sketch, or extemporaneous. The important thing is to use *you*, *you*, *you* and get away from saying "I." Make them feel that you believe they are important.

Small Mistakes

Early in the talk the danger of making a small mistake is more likely than it is later, after you get into the "groove" and have your audience moving along with you. If you have practiced the skills of public speaking and audience control, you will have them with you all the way. If a small mistake is made, even in grammar, don't bother to correct it. Watch that it does not happen again.

If it is a glaring mistake that would have a tendency to put doubt in their mind as to numbers or statistics or facts, then correct it as you go quickly, and move on. Do not let the mistake get you into a state of doubt for then the audience will surely doubt your credibility. It is extremely important that you avoid mistakes and the mistake of compounding them in the beginning of the speech.

Shake Hands with Your Audience

In the early part of your talk, as you begin to magnify your central theme and get into your speech, you should figuratively shake hands with your audience. Tell them you're glad to be there and be sure in stating your central theme to offer some profit for them personally if they listen to what you are about to say. By all means it may be well to use a line that indicates your talk is not only going to be informative, educational, and possibly inspiring to them, but you feel it is also going to be enjoyable.

The audience simply does not want to anticipate in the early part of the talk that they must sit in their seats and listen to something that may not be very interesting or, more importantly, may not be delivered in such a way that will hold their interest. In short, the audience really wants you to succeed. They do not want to be in an audience where a speaker fails to deliver, or fails to get and hold their attention. It is boring, it is time consuming, and they simply are not interested in that kind of a program.

Keep this in mind as you begin giving your central theme and magnifying that central theme.

Large or Outdoor Audiences

When you are speaking to an extremely large group, it is necessary to start off a little slower than with a small audience. You automatically shift into the necessary gear to grab and hold the attention of the audience. When you start off slowly, whatever you do, do not fade later; keep firing away, and as you get further into your speech your rate of speech will automatically pick up. You will pick up speed and fluency, and your audience will take in your ideas faster. Stories and examples are clearly spelled out because you took the trouble to ease into your talk.

Do not be too hasty, move along slowly, be deliberate, be direct, be assuring. When you appear to be in a hurry, it could mean that you are a little too apprehensive of the occasion or it could also mean that deep down inside you do not feel qualified to be there. It could even mean that you do not pay enough respect to this particular occasion to give it your best. You may seem to be in a hurry to get somewhere else. Move along slowly as you get into your speech and begin to get hold of your audience.

Make Worthwhile Suggestions

In order to deliver a meaningful speech, the facts, the points you make, and the direction you suggest must all be solid and meaningful to the audience. There is no need to give ideas to an audience that they can do nothing about. Keep in mind that when someone is talking to you about better government, about how to make government work better for you and all people, they usually end by telling you what you can do about it. You can become informed. You can go to the polls and you can work for and speak for the person of your choice. You can exercise your right to vote, your right to choose. This is one of many examples of how you must state your central theme. Have your subject built around something the audience can do something about, unless of course it is only to inform and no action is needed at the time. It would still be very poor speaking skill not to have some suggestions toward the end of your talk.

Conversational Speech

Many times articles on better speech making tell you to speak as if you are engaged in a conversation. This is very true, particularly for small groups. This is not so true if it is an audience of thousands. It is also very true in the early part of a talk as you give your central theme, as you begin to drive home the importance of your central theme. Conversational style at the top of a speech is very effective. But as you get further into your speech and become more enthusiastic about it, you begin to gesture more freely; as you begin to live the words you are speaking and put real meaning into what you say and how you say it, you will become more of a showman.

It will be less conversational, so don't be afraid to put a little show in your talk, provided you feel it and know the subject well enough to make this come about. Your friendliness must be genuine, your approach to your audience must be poised and easy. If you are merely putting on a show for the purpose of appearing to be a showman, your audience will know it and resent it, and they will turn you off.

Get 'em in Trouble, Get 'em Out

All drama begins with getting the hero in trouble. It gives a reason for becoming interested in what is happening and for what is going to happen next. In the middle of this drama are examples to support the fact that the hero is in trouble. This same method applies to good effective speech delivery. Get your audience in trouble by citing the problems they are having. People problems are usually good subjects to cover. No one loves a problem like their own. Get 'em in trouble and then point out how they can overcome these obstacles, how they can get out of trouble if they will take your advice. Whatever you do, do not get your audience in trouble and fail to suggest how to get them out. To some extent this deals with speech preparation, but it is important that it be mentioned here.

Be animated about it if you are spelling out the problems of economy. Use language that lets them know that it is your problem, too. If you are talking about the problem of today's employees not being as ambitious and as energetic as they once were, (this is heard often), then be sure you let them know that it applies to you. Give examples. You may tell how you were treated at the front desk of a major hotel and point out that this condition is with us and is likely to continue unless we do certain things. Point out that not only do they have troubles, but their competitors are having the same type of people problems. This becomes meaningful to them and they see that you are telling them something to make them realize why they are there. You must offer some solution, some hope. Never leave your audience without hope.

State Hard Facts

In magnifying your central theme, you may want to state hard facts as a means of getting their attention. For example, you could quote the latest crime figures by saying something like: "Twenty-one major crimes are committed in the United States every minute. Every minute in the United States there are ten burglaries. Every minute in the United States there is a forceable rape." Pause between these statements to let them sink in. You're using numbers and it's important that you let them sink in before getting on to the next important fact or the beginning of your talk. Look at your full audience. See if they heard you. See if it registers in their faces. When you state hard facts such as these to an audience, the impact will reflect in their eyes. You'll see the reaction in their faces. Then immediately give what you think can be done about this subject; what they can do to curb rampant crime in the United States.

Hard facts are also startling facts. Few people realize that the crime situation has gotten so badly out of hand. Later on in the talk those same figures may and probably should be used again.

You have reached down into the middle of your speech to pull out something that is startling and shocking to use to capture their attention. In other words, you have gotten them in trouble. You will support that trouble with facts; then all you have to do is get them safely out. Quite often today people and audiences have so many problems of their own that their minds are off somewhere wondering and worrying about these problems. A clever and skillful speaker can bring the minds of the audience members into the meeting room and keep them there during the entire time of his or her talk if he or she learns and practices the power of audience control.

This is opening your talk with impact. This is getting your adrenalin flowing and the audience's as well. This is tying that audience to you; it is making them see that you have something important to say and that you are prepared to say it well. Rest assured that if you deliver this type of opening with real impact you will get their attention and you will keep it.

Emphasize Your Main Purpose

The main purpose of your speech—it could be a "how-to-speech" or a programmed speech—is to give the audience what they've been promised. You must lead into that from the top. Here is where you make the main thrust. Constantly keep before them the main purpose of your being there, what you are trying to accomplish, and the fact that you have some worthwhile thoughts on it.

The late Elmer Wheeler in his book, *Tested Public Speaking*, said that the topic of your speech should be like a rope, a steel rope, that runs through your speech entirely. Occasionally you may repeat a statement or a phrase that calls their attention to what you have stated at the beginning of your speech.

You need to know how to relate to it. If, when you speak of enthusiasm and inspiration, you could say, "If you are enthusiastic then you have a good attitude," then you're relating. This would be a motivational-type talk to salespeople or even to a convention group. *Attitude* is so important; Earl Nightingale calls attitude the magic word.

The difference is that when giving an inspirational talk, you tell your audience that, "The difference between an amateur and a pro is that an amateur gets there and sees that the job looks tough, so he says, 'I'll wait until it's easier.' Conversely, the pro gets there and says, 'Regardless of today's circumstances, I'm committed and I'm going to make it happen because that's my job.' " That's attitude. Then you could discuss attitude and how it relates to being enthusiastic.

You now begin to point out what you are going to cover, how you are going to help your audience be more enthusiastic themselves, and how to get others around them to be more enthusiastic, as you would a management group.

State Your Belief

It is important for you to state your central theme and your feelings about it. Later on in the body of your talk and in the summary you can come back to this and let your audience know that you see this problem as they do, that you are doing something about it or intend to do something about it, and ask them to do likewise. Too often you hear a speaker who never makes it quite clear what his or her stand is on a particular subject. If you have an objective you can say it in one sentence, and you certainly need to let them know where you stand.

Keep in mind that you are constantly trying to get your audience to think along with you as you speak. If you can get the audience to think with you, you gain control of their thinking. One of the key factors here is to let them know exactly how you feel and how you think on this particular part of your subject. If they know how you feel and think, you can hope to have them thinking the same way and continue from point to point as you deliver and make the most of the power of audience control.

If you are talking to a business group and the subject is inflation, for example, you could make point after point about how inflation is affecting you and your total income. You could point out what the grocery bill has become over a period of five years. You could talk about the cost of new automobiles. Both examples fit every audience. Now you are getting into the main part of the speech but these could easily be a part of your opening statement. It is important that you spell these out in a simple way that fits both you and the audience.

It wouldn't be very wise to talk gross national product with a group of unsophisticated but hard-working and professional salespeople. They're generally not very concerned with the gross national product. Talk to them about buyer resistance and what can be done about it. Talk to them about persistence in making their sales calls . . . the mark of the true professional. The point is that all of these can be intertwined when you magnify your central theme. You get 'em in trouble and get 'em out. You have to plan this carefully to be sure that what you are promising will be delivered.

Forget Yourself

You have their attention. You are beginning to get into your talk. Now magnify your central theme; state it first, then magnify it with an example, an anecdote, a point, a question, or any of these methods. Then get into the subject and begin to point out just why you have that subject and it is your central theme. Now it's up to you, your preparations, and your delivery.

"Thinking on your feet" becomes more and more meaningful as you progress. Thinking on your feet means you think of how you are getting your message across, not of how you look or how you appear to that audience. That has already been determined and should have been taken care of much earlier, so quit worrying about it now. Begin to think in terms of the actual delivery of your central theme.

Call for Better Citizenship

The mayor of a sizeable city addressed an important local civic club, and called for better day-to-day citizenship. To get his people, particularly this group, to become more civic-minded, he stated his central theme and magnified that central theme to be sure they were with him all the way.

He told them that:

> "The news media has been reporting a great deal about the energy crisis because it's a prime concern to all of us, and without this energy our power problems become paramount." He quickly reviewed the sources of power throughout the history of the United States, "Steam, then oil, then nuclear power, and finally the marketing era of economic power, helped make America the power of the world. While they're important to the historian and the economist, many of us overlook the real power source of America's greatness, people power!"

In that talk, once he set the stage, he magnified the fact that people power—their voting, their being informed, their being concerned, their attempting to do the right and correct thing—would solve any and all problems that his city or any other city could possibly have. He ended his speech with a call for action on their part and received a standing ovation because it was an important subject covered extremely well.

He stated his central theme. He then magnified his central theme by making comparisons as to various kinds of power. This was an effective speech because these techniques were used in a dramatic manner.

Here is another good example of a speaker addressing a civic group, stating his theme, and magnifying it. He named the founder of that organization and said,

> *If he could come back to life he would say to me today, don't talk to them about the past, but talk to them about the future and the opportunity and challenge that we have and then tell them what they can do about it.*

Briefly, the speaker stated and magnified his central theme. The audience knew what to expect. They knew that they were going to be reminded of the problems of our time and how they might help to solve those problems. This was brief and short, but he was into his speech and while they may not have felt that they needed to be reminded, it was a means for stating in a unique way what that organization was founded on, its philosophy, and why it was important to rethink it from time to time. He wanted to inspire that group to continue to achieve.

The AIDA Formula

Through selling, a formula called AIDA is often used to lead and inspire people. **A** is for attention . . . already discussed, **I** is for interest . . . covered in this chapter, **D** is for desire and **A** is for action . . . both to be covered in later chapters.

Although they really did not come to hear only stories, audiences usually like a message with humor. You cannot forget their interest. State the central theme and magnify it forcefully. If this is not done, then you certainly cannot expect to get their interest. After all, the program stated what your subject is. The subject is probably repeated in your introduction. Now you must magnify that subject in various ways to get that interest. This is the *interest* step.

You know that the audience must be attentive if control is to be attained. Now you must capture their complete interest if you are to maintain that control. You must be constantly aware of the danger of losing control of the audience at every transition point in your speech. Lose control and you lose the power it provides.

Then get further into this formula and talk about creating a desire on their part, then a call for action. The AIDA formula can be used here to magnify your central theme as you put to use the interest step.

Another Formula

A procedure somewhat like the AIDA formula, one that is in four steps, is (1) present the problem, (2) offer the solution, (3) prove your case, (4) then call for action.

This is the first phase of this formula: to present the problem. You do this by stating and magnifying your central theme. The passage about the crime rate today in America certainly does magnify the problem. It drives home the point that we're living in dangerous times. Any speaker covering that subject would obviously go on to prove his or her case by giving example after example of what is happening across America, ending with a call for action. This is another method of preparing, and also of delivering your talk. When you have prepared and are ready to deliver, it does not matter what method you use to deliver. The *method* of delivery is unimportant, but you must keep these four steps in mind, or you will not be properly prepared.

Humorist's Theme

I talked in terms of speeches being for one of three purposes—to inform, to inspire or to entertain. Regardless of the first two, whether it's totally for briefing and information or an inspiring call for action, the central theme must be stated at the top. The one exception might be the humorous speech.

Now, if an audience has come to hear the speaker who has been billed through advance notice and publicity as being a humorist, such as an after-dinner speaker, they do not expect a serious message. About the only way the humorous speaker who is going to keep us laughing uses the central theme is to state something like:

> *You know, I'm here tonight to take part in your program, hopefully to give you an enjoyable next few moments. I don't have a great message and I don't pretend to. I'm here to give you a few laughs, to help you look at life a little differently, and if I succeed in making you laugh a little bit and forget your worries, then I have succeeded in my mission.*

Now that is magnifying the central theme. It doesn't have a specific theme, but it is a specific reason for the speaker being there. He or she goes on to tell you in a few words that laughter is what you need, that it is the best therapy in the world, and he or she makes no apologies for his or her efforts to make people laugh and to forget some of their problems.

Chances are the humorist will acknowledge the introduction with more humor than suggested here for the typical speech. Possibly he or she will have a few more quips while addressing the audience, then he or she will begin to think about using anecdotes, humorous stories, and one-liners to keep it humorous all the way.

The humorist may break it up occasionally with a mild message in between the humor, and that mild message will serve more than anything as a transition point before he or she is back again telling stories. One very famous after-dinner speaker promises his audiences at least a belly-laugh a minute. . . .

* * * * *

Now—you're involved!

5

Tested Techniques
for Getting
Audience Involvement

Getting them to go along . . .

In order to succeed with a speech of any kind you must first get the audience involved with the message you are about to deliver. They cannot become interested until they become involved. Getting the audience involved is not accidental, it is planned. You don't hope for it; it isn't a hit or miss situation; it simply is good wording of your theme that you have magnified already. Get the wording so that the audience will have a sort of chemistry with you, a rapport between audience and speaker.

Many speech trainers say that if you do not get the audience's attention in the first three minutes, you might just as well pack up and leave, as far as any really successful speech delivery is concerned. This may be a bit exaggerated, but certainly if you do not get them involved or interested in the first three minutes, you will either struggle for quite some time to get them involved or you may miss totally.

Emotion

Emotional speaking is a clever technique on the part of the speaker, provided, of course, he or she has an emotional feeling for the subject and can then tie it in successfully to the audience, to their purposes and to their hopes. This is done by using various speech techniques such as the *stage whisper*. Ty Boyd, CPAE, past president of National Speakers Association, is a master at the stage whisper. When he puts the stage whisper technique to use, you can hear it in the back of the room, just as if he were speaking in a normal tone of voice. This comes from his many years of experience as a broadcaster and a telecaster, but he uses this ability to make great use of a stage whisper. It works wonders for him in displaying his feelings as he displays emotion in his inspiring talks.

Direct Statement

A straightforward statement as to what you are going to talk about and how it fits the audience is probably the most basic method of audience involvement and probably is used more than any other single method.

Let's see how this could be used in a typical company sales meeting. It doesn't necessarily have to be a large company, but a company where the speakers participating in the program are members of the staff. This is a very popular method of getting subjects covered by those on the speaking team. It has the value of getting the speakers more involved in the subjects assigned them. But, of course, they must be selected on their feeling for and their ability to do the thing that you assign them to do, or it loses credibility. Here are the opening statements of such a meeting by a salesperson who is an exceptionally good representative, concerning servicing the accounts:

> *I have been asked to discuss briefly with you a subject that I feel is of utmost importance . . . if (and he emphasized "if") we (and he emphasized "we") do our job in the way that will have the most effect on those with whom we come in contact, the things that will make us entirely different from just ordinary salespeople . . . and will set us apart from our competitors, can be summed up in a very few words—improving sales through better service.*

He goes on to say as a follow-up of that opening statement in which "we" is emphasized and by implying that he's putting himself into that same category, that:

> *Service is the very essence of our existence. In these United States, with our industry as competitive as it is, with millions of dollars being spent each year on all types of advertising, promotion, and gimmicks, our only weapon against our largest competitors is that of service with quality merchandise.*

You can see that he has repeated. He has begun to point out what service really is and how important it is after having already said in the first paragraph, that this would be his company's sure method for being competitive with larger companies and probably with those who have products just as good. That's a very astute statement on the part of this particular salesperson.

Seminar Workshop

The seminar-workshop type of meeting is somewhat different in that it is designed and programmed for feedback from the group. This type of meeting will be discussed in a later chapter; however, it goes without saying that even if feedback is planned, you have to establish a rapport, you have to establish involvement, or there is no reason to be there making statements and asking questions. The more you know about your audience, the easier it is to establish rapport and promote feedback.

Seminar groups differ in their willingness to participate in discussion. This may not necessarily be your fault as the speaker. However, it does not free you from the obligation of getting feedback and discussion, because without this interplay between speaker and audience, and between various members of the group, there is no reason to label this meeting as a seminar or workshop. As the leader, you must re-examine the steps you have taken so far in gaining their attention. Possibly say something forceful to attempt to get that attention rekindled. If not, it becomes a lecture . .   and your control will be lost.

Statement-Definition

Here is a method for getting the attention of the audience and quickly tying it in with the members of that audience. The title of the speech is called *Sterility*, or barren. This type of talk could be delivered to a professional group such as a group of marketers, advertisers, promotion experts, public relations professionals, or any group that consists of pooled professional efforts for its own professional improvement. This is a talk meant to inspire the professionals to do a better job of managing their affairs.

You could use this sentence, "Sterility in business and management is our subject." It could continue something like this:

> *Throughout the length and breadth of our land, there are business firms, both large and small, which constantly hang on the fringe of stability and success. There are others that each year sink down into oblivion and fail. There are others that show little progress each year, but whose growth records are like undernourished plants.*

They grow enough to keep alive but never seem to develop the strong and hearty physique that would make them independent of circumstances.

All right, let's say this is a convention. Let's say that you are asked to address them in an inspirational manner, to talk about the true techniques, the prerequisites for success in their field of endeavor. You can quickly see that it's a universal-type subject, and a universal approach that can be taken.

You can follow up that original statement by saying,

There's another group of firms far more limited, but with phenomenal growth records. Their position is the envy of others. These firms have strength and productiveness in their overall success patterns. What makes these so much more successful than others?

Then you could answer the question this way:

This magic ingredient that makes some companies become great and successful is available to all companies within their industries, and within this industry. We all have access to it—everyone actually possesses this. However, all too often it is kept a prisoner rather than put to use as a winning serve. This magic element is the mind of man. Now since we all own this powerful force, why is there such a difference in the success picture of competitive men? The battle for greatness doesn't come with product location or prestige.

Those are good starts to be sure. Then continue:

"The real battle is a battle of survival on the basis of man against man, the one who employs the best use of his mind. Against competition that man would be the one who would come out ahead in the long run."

Now this may seem to be something of a trite start, but it

is a way for you to get into your program. It could have a little
more zip, a little more of a dynamic approach by employing
various methods, but if a pure statement of fact is all that you
feel qualified to use to establish this involvement, then it's all
right. Here you cannot see in the written words how much
actual strength can be gained from such an opening because
you don't actually hear the words being said. You don't get to
see the body language, or facial expressions, or hear the tone
of voice that drives home these seemingly trite remarks. Rest
assured, the polished, accomplished speaker can breathe a
lot of life into these seemingly trite remarks.

Then you could go on and cover the points that are
established, proving to the audience that the strength really
lies in the one on one, man against man situation—not a bad
opening for establishing some sort of rapport. Notice in that
first statement you used the analogy of an undernourished
plant. Later in the speech you could go on and say that those
who succeed offer nourishment to their ideas, to their total
concept and philosophy of business. More importantly, they
offer nourishment to the people within the company. You
could easily prove the point by saying that this nourishment
could be the difference in mind against mind, man against
man situations.

When you can develop a rapport with an audience about
the value of "one on one" interaction with others, you can
easily establish an individual involvement with you and
your subject. The above speech passage shows how to deliver with real feeling, and how to get the audience involved
with you and your message. With this close feeling about a
common interest (leadership) an audience becomes totally
involved. This involvement translates to the real power of
audience control.

The You Approach

A lawyer uses this in the summary to the jury. The
lawyer appeals with the *you approach* to the people of the

jury and involves that jury. It is a speech in itself, as those who have ever heard a skilled lawyer or district attorney sum up a case will recognize. He or she can point out to the jurors how the burden of guilt rests with them, and can remind them, in the case of a defense attorney, that they don't want to have this guilt on their minds. A prosecuting district attorney will remind the jury that they certainly don't want to release without punishment a person who has committed these crimes. It is a very forceful way of using the you approach in a speech.

Here is another good way to use the you approach. This is taken from the opening remarks of a United States senator addressing a western state's association of bankers.

> *Being with you this afternoon reminds me of the time when one of my hometown bankers was approached on the street by a seedy looking character with the shakes, asking for a handout. My good friend reached into his pocket and pressed a bill into the man's hand. "See that you get some food with this," my friend said. The seedy looking recipient immediately got indignant and said, "My dear sir, do I tell you what to do with your money?"*

You can see that this politician was, in a sense, relating to the group of bankers in the audience that he too has obligations relating to money, through legislation and that sort of thing. The next paragraph is where he really ties it in with something that is very much the you approach:

> *Having been through a couple of successful campaigns, I have found that bankers and their personnel are very good at politics. They campaign clean and fair but intensely, and they are extremely competitive. But you know, I have found that it is characteristic of politics in our state to be clean and fair, but intense.*

He went on then to tell about bad situations of dirty

politics in other areas and talked with a sense of pride about their state. This senator knew how to tie in the you factor in order to get the audience involved with his message.

Rhetorical Questions

The rhetorical question is a technique widely used in large audiences. You merely ask questions. The answers should favorably tie in your audience to you and what you have to say as you proceed to deliver your message.

Here's a talk delivered at a sales and marketing association by a salesperson who talked to them on the subject of what a salesperson should be:

> What makes one salesperson famous and outstanding and another unknown? Why is it that some salespeople can close three plus out of every five contracts and others close only two out of ten? Why? In your business or industry why do you have salespeople who stand out head and shoulders above the others? Is there any key to be known? How do successful business people, successful salespeople, differ from ordinary people? Are they any better or worse?

The speaker went into an explanation of how the answer to these questions appeared to be unknown, and he began to think about it. Here are his remarks as to how he felt:

> I have found that most people are interested in successful businesspeople and successful salespeople and sincerely wonder how they differ from the neighbors next door.
>
> Also, after talking to a lot of people, such as presidents of companies, sales managers, clerks and just down-to-earth people, I've come to wonder myself how they were different and why they were different. Do they have anything in common, these people who stick out from the crowd for one

*reason or another, who stand for one hour, or a day,
or a lifetime in the spotlight? Here are a few tentative conclusions I have reached.*

Then he gave the answer as to what he had found out based
on his day-to-day research into the subject; it was less a
matter of talent than concentration. He went on to say that
the power of concentration, the ability to give attention to a
fixed goal or situation, was the surest avenue to becoming
successful in selling.

Now he wasn't the first speaker, sales trainer or sales
manager who had determined this. Successful selling by the
experts is caused by concentration and the point can be
proved. His unique way of getting into the subject so that he
could answer the questions that he had posed was a tried and
true method of getting the audience involved with the subject about to be discussed.

This speaker continued on to tell how this matter of
concentration plus the other ingredients that must go with it
had answered the question for him. It had meaning and in
sharing this answer he served the audience, which was his
primary reason for being on the program.

Humorous Rapport

To gain control with humor, you must first realize that
the audience needs a common interest and that your remarks
must be interesting if you are to get their attention. Here are
the remarks by a speaker who spoke on behalf of his own
church and the members of that group, with a somewhat
humorous approach to it.

*A burglar, who had entered a poor minister's
house at midnight, tripped over a chair and woke
the minister. Drawing his knife, the burglar said,
"If you yell for help, you're a dead man. I'm hunting for money." The minister said, "Let me get up
and strike a light and I'll hunt with you."*

You see, the point was astutely made so that the speaker could go on then to talk about the money the church needed—a humorous tie-in, and a humorous approach to audience involvement.

Let us suppose that you as a speaker did not use any of the one-liners, the quick techniques described in Chapters 1 and 3 of this book. Let's assume that you merely acknowledged your introduction, recognized those who should be mentioned in your opening address, and began your speech. You could start right at the top with this humorous tie-in and go right on raising money for the church. It could be used for raising money for the YMCA or YWCA. It has many uses— it's a humorous story that leads right into the purpose of your talk.

A Unique Statement

Here are the opening remarks of a mayor giving a commencement address to a group in a small university in the Deep South:

> These remarks are intended for those who are willing to take stock of themselves, who will pause to plan for tomorrow . . . to consider a span of years, perhaps through the final quarter of this century. We all can comprehend such a period of time but, with few exceptions, will hardly anticipate the many marvelous changes that will affect our lives. For that matter, change is already coming at such an accelerated pace, it's breathtaking in comparison to the past.

Notice the questions that any person would be asking themselves. The group is asked to comprehend the future. Notice how the mayor says, "that will affect our lives." Then the mayor goes on to talk about change at an accelerated pace and how change makes it important for those of us who take stock of ourselves and plan for tomorrow.

Point after point is made on behalf of those who want to recognize the fact that the so-called commencement of a graduating class is in fact the beginning of their entire future. Young people have to be reminded of this even though it may not seem necessary at the time.

A Unique Comparison

Here's another example of an opening statement a speaker used in a unique way,

> *Square pegs don't go in round holes because they won't give a little. They're rigid, inflexible, and set in their ways. They do not possess adaptability.*

The name of this particular talk is called "Give a Little." It's a talk about human relations . . . about getting along with others. The speaker points out that everything has to give a little in the field of human relations. In interaction with other people we all have to give ground a little bit. The speaker doesn't ask you to compromise your convictions, just to be flexible and to give a little.

The speaker uses a good example of catching a baseball going at 75 miles an hour without injuring your hand. He points out that a good professional baseball fielder catches balls at this rate of speed by giving a little as the ball hits the glove. And anyone who has ever played baseball knows how true that is.

Special Interest Narrative

This is used as a narrative opening in order to establish rapport and get the audience involved:

> *Several years ago the afternoon train pulled into a small Quaker town in Pennsylvania. As it stopped a stranger swung off the train. He walked over to one of the people on the platform and*

asked, "What type of town is this and what kind of people live here?" The local townsman looked him in the eye and asked, "What kind of place did you come from and what were the people like who lived there?" The stranger then replied to the Quaker, "They were hard people to get along with and the town was noisy." Without hesitation the Quaker told the stranger, "This is the same kind of town and the same kind of people live here." So the stranger got back on the train.

The next afternoon when the train pulled in, off popped another stranger. Smiling, he approached the group of local Quakers on the platform and cheerily said, "Hi there. I'm looking for a town to live in permanently. What do you have here?" Once more the Quaker replied, "Where did you come from and what were the people like?" In the same happy tone the stranger said, "I came from a happy place; the people were kind and friendly." Without hesitation the Quaker told him, "You'll find the same kind of people here."

Know what the special interests of your audience will be. It could be professionalism, civic matters, tax reduction, or self-motivation. It could be a group with more than one special interest. When this special interest is known by you, it is an easy matter to appeal to that interest and to get involvement; provided, of course, you have those same feelings about, or understand those interests. If not, then you should not be on that program to begin with. You cannot get audience involvement through insincere, fraudulent methods.

Never Talk Down

Talking down to an audience is a sure way to turn off any willingness of the audience to get involved. This is a real danger in the early part of a speech, particularly when you are trying to establish your credibility. Leave this to your introduction, and if not properly done, be extremely careful in giving your own credits.

Management people tend to talk down to their sales team as they get into their talk. There is no such thing as a captive audience. You can force employees to sit there in a meeting, you can force them to be quiet and appear to be listening, but you cannot force them to open their minds to your message. This calls for audience involvement, and the skilled speaker can achieve this rapport. When this real interest, this mental involvement has been established, the power of audience control can begin . . . and not before.

The "I" Trip

Everyone has seen personalities, stars, etc., interviewed, who never got away from talking about themselves, the "I" syndrome. Most people turn off the interview, physically or mentally. No matter who the speaker is, the audience must be involved or it simply will not think along with the speaker.

Recently the athletic director of a well-known university addressed a group of area businesspeople, all of whom enjoyed a degree of success in their own fields. He talked for more than ten minutes about himself, how he applied his own self-motivation, the books he had read, and in general how he got to be such a big man.

His talk was recorded and then transcribed. It was amazing to see how many times the personal pronoun was used. About half-way through the fourth page of the manuscript he finally said "we," apparently attempting to establish some form of audience involvement. He probably could have, but his ego got in the way and he was right back on his favorite word . . . I.

His talk could be rated as a bomb. His university should send another representative to the next meeting of this kind . . . or else enlighten him on the techniques of effective speaking. . . .

*****

Don't praise yourself, let others do it!

6

How to Deliver
Like a Pro
and Still Be Yourself

But an improved self . . .

Effective delivery of a good speech begins the moment you stand up. How you appear as you start your speech is very important and, remember, you will be observed even before you begin to speak. You must be yourself. Your appearance is extremely important. You must be a speaker well prepared, well versed on your subject; the *whole person* delivers!

A study of Jimmy Carter's platform appearance, his platform presence, and his delivery during his campaign for the Presidency of the United States was made. Many things were reported, but the most important thing of all was that Jimmy Carter gave *credibility* to his subject. Even though he was unprofessional as a speaker, this unprofessionalism had a tendency to work in his favor. His sincerity and, therefore, his delivery, was believable.

Making a speech is somewhat like selling. You are selling an audience an idea. It is very obvious that if you do not believe what you are saying, if you are not sincere, you cannot fool the audience Therefore, the first step must be *preparation.* If you do not believe in the subject you are to cover, you will not be able to sell it to the audience. You will not be sincere and the audience will sense this right away.

Naturally, the very beginning of your speech is the best time to make a good impression. Get control at the start. It would be an overstatement to say that a speaker can't overcome a poor first impression, but it is difficult to overcome a poor first impression. Do not start off in a weak and inadequate way to deliver the message. You must be prepared so that you can immediately get into your speech, take charge, and gain early control!

Never Apologize

Speech teachers and professional speakers agree that one of the worst things a speaker can do is to apologize for anything: for having a bad cold; for having difficulty in getting to the meeting place; for being a little late; even for not having enough time to prepare properly. The audience is not interested and will not listen to excuses or alibis. You've been properly introduced and now it's time to deliver; leave off all apologies.

Support the Entire Program

Another unpardonable sin is to be critical of the very program in which you are participating. Remember that all speakers on a program should do all in their power to make the full program successful. When one speaker is critical of how the program is unfolding, or how the time is going, or how his or her time slot on the program is misplaced, it has a negative effect on the audience and all concerned.

Be Self-Assured

Never talk yourself down by self-criticism. To show humility is all right, but don't overdo it. You often hear speakers who comment that they really aren't suited for such an occasion, but that they will do the best they can. An audience is not interested in that kind of attitude. A speaker may also get up and say, "I've been given this spot on the program, but I'm not sure that some of you don't know more about it than I do." This is a very negative approach that is uncalled for and detrimental.

Don't Be Commercial

Another sin is when a speaker gets up and begins to sell himself, his product, or his service to the audience. This is in very poor taste. Chances are you have been listed properly in the program, giving your company or your organization proper credit, and if so, there is no need to further sell yourself. That is commercializing.

You've heard speakers get up and begin to tell about all the places at which they spoke yesterday or the day before. This is of no real interest to the audience. This type of travelogue might have been interesting in Mark Twain's day when travel was not as widespread as it is today, but most of your audience has been everywhere that you've been.

Avoid Being Pompous

Talking down to an audience is as bad or worse than being too apologetic and humble. In your premeeting analysis you should have determined a great deal about your audience, their educational level, their financial levels, etc. The important point here is not to talk down to your audience. Deliver your speech in a straightforward manner. You have something to say to this group or you should not be there. It is a matter of not trying to be the big shot, of not trying to be something that you are not. The important thing is to be yourself and to constantly aim at improving yourself as a person and as a speaker. In this way you avoid being too positive or too negative.

Speak Up

Most speakers should talk louder than normal. Trained speakers have voices that carry well, and you will notice that the professional speakers usually talk a little louder than their normal conversational style. This has several effects. First of all it puts a little more excitement into their words. It gives an opportunity to soften the voice as you change pace, which is extremely effective. You can change pitch or lower your voice for emphasis. You may want to start off very low and very soft, then gradually increase your volume as you get into your message. Too much volume can be overdone, so be extremely careful that you don't talk too loudly. If in doubt, a good rule to follow is to talk a little louder than normal, even with a PA system.

Talking too softly when delivering a speech tends to make it seem less forceful. Obviously if you were giving a eulogy this would not apply. It would be delivered in a softer, less forceful manner. But most speakers have a message to deliver—ideas to share with the audience, possibly some action to be started because of their appearance. If you talk too softly there will be those who cannot hear you in the back of the room. Guard against this by talking a little louder than you normally would.

This is not meant to be a passage concerning good voice. If you are a frequent speaker and need some voice coaching, by all means, get it. It can make a huge difference in your delivery. You could go to a high-school voice teacher, a nearby choir director, or a professional voice coach. The best method of determining what you need is to get a tape and replay your talk after you have delivered it to an audience. This will help you to find your voice weaknesses if you have any. You can also study your timing, which will be explained later. A voice can hardly be too low but a high-pitched voice doesn't come over a microphone well. It tends to have a shrieking sound to it.

Proper Breathing

Learn to breathe deeply and frequently. This comes with experience, but it can be studied with improvements made. After you have practiced good breathing habits it will be no problem and will become your normal breathing.

Make it a habit to breathe deeply several times just before you begin to speak. You can do this as you are waiting to be introduced, or as you are being introduced. Take several deep breaths. Don't try to do this after you have started. It would seem rather unusual for a speaker to get up and begin to try to breathe deeply as he or she makes his or her first few remarks after being introduced.

Speak Clearly

Learn to make *each syllable* stand out in your words. Quite often you hear a speaker who will let one or more syllables fall, or as the speech teachers refer to it, *voice endings* in which a final syllable doesn't come through. Sometimes this can change the entire meaning of a word, a sentence, or even the total passage. Learn to sound your syllables. One of the most effective habits you can acquire to become a more forceful speaker is to read aloud. Set aside some time as you begin to develop as a speaker for doing nothing but reading aloud. Make your syllables and full words stand out. Even reading someone else's writing can help you to see what the most important words are in a sentence and help you to emphasize those words.

Avoid anything that appears to be akin to an *oratory*. Chances are you are not going to be delivering a speech that calls for the type of oratory you've read about in history, talks of William Jennings Bryan and the famous speakers of his time. They didn't have PA systems in those days and speaking called for more oratorical methods than today.

Avoid Nasality

Learn to avoid any *nasality*. Speakers who have a nasal sound in their voices are irritating to an audience. They simply do not sound good. This, too, can be corrected through better breathing techniques. Learning to breathe from your diaphragm, your belly, instead of from your lungs, will help avoid this nasality. A voice teacher can recommend voice exercises that will help you to correct this nasal sound in your speaking.

Avoid Monotone

Probably the most boring delivery of all that any speaker can get into is the monotone sound. Some speakers never change their pitch; they never go high or low; they never change their speed of delivery. It's one sound coming out constantly, almost in a sing-song manner. Learn to eliminate this monotone by changing pitch, lowering your voice, raising your voice, and changing speed.

Changing speed of delivery is probably one of the easiest things to correct and use. You simply talk faster at times and slow down at other times, usually for emphasis. One of the most effective techniques of skilled spakers is the use of the *pause*. Don't be afraid to pause between statements. It has the effect of emphasis and it works. The speaker's pause in his or her delivery is considered by many to be one of the most valuable techniques in speaking. It may also be the most neglected. A pause gets full attention. A pause can help you to get and maintain audience control. In fact, the pause technique can help a speaker to regain control if it appears to be slipping away.

Pausing

Here are some general rules for pausing. Pausing is to some extent timing. As you know, all comedians talk about getting their timing. Timing is important to anyone who delivers words to an audience of any kind: actor, stand-up comic, public speaker. Occasionally you will hear someone say his or her timing is off. Pausing will have more effect in improving timing than any other one thing. Here are some suggestions:

1. Group together words that express an idea or thought. Separate these groups one from another by a pause.

2. Pausing may be used to emphasize a single word. Pause before the word and after the word.

3. Pausing can be used to show meaning. Proper pausing will emphasize what the real meaning of your words are.

4. It's important that you learn to pause and to breathe while you are pausing. This helps to strengthen your delivery. You have to learn to breathe and the pause is the proper place to do it.

5. The larger your audience, the longer the pause. Of course, like everything else, there are some limitations to this statement. Obviously, if you were addressing a group of thousands—five, six, or seven thousand is not uncommon in today's meetings and convention programs—you would not exaggerate the length of the pause over that used in speaking to a group of 50, but the pause for the larger audience should be longer than for a smaller group.

Veteran speech trainer J. W. Morris of Atlanta says, "Skill in the use of the pause may be a speaker's most effective technique."

In a small group the pause is more like a stop in the conversation, but in a big audience, with so many more people hearing and being affected by what you have to say, the longer pause is more necessary. It may even be wise to mark your notes for good places to pause. After a while it becomes second nature and you will realize, without having to think about it, where it's important to pause, how long to pause, and how frequently to pause. It depends on your message and your feeling for it.

Be Pleasant

Put a smile in your voice. How can a person make strong positive statements without feeling good about those statements? And if it's something you can feel good about, then you can smile as you make your delivery. This is not meant just for the humorous talk or funny passages in a talk. The telephone company teaches their operators to put a smile into their voices as they talk to people on the telephone. One of the first rules of telephone selling, which has become extremely popular in recent years, is to teach the salesperson to have a smile in his or her voice. If you've had some telephone solicitations, you realize how very pleasant and how effective a good telephone voice can be. If it works for them, it certainly works for any speaker.

Think back to the halcyon days of radio. Some people on radio sounded very, very effective simply because they could put a smile in their voice. It's difficult to do at times, but except for a passage in your speech where you want to become somewhat forceful, or want to ask for real action and mean to be quite serious, a smile in your voice will reap big dividends because it makes for easier listening. The audience will like you and appreciate you as a pleasant person.

It stands to reason that if an audience likes you (some do . . . some don't seem to) and if an audience appreciates your effort . . . they will be listening. It is hard to picture a person in the audience not listening, not paying attention, if that person likes the speaker. If they like you, and you continue to merit their appreciation, you have a real power working for you . . . the power of audience control.

Focus on the Audience

The mood of an audience can change during a speech and the skillful speaker will detect this change and adjust accordingly. This does not mean that the speaker must change his or her material. The professional *could* do this, but it's not likely to be necessary. When the mood changes and you should change, that simply means to change delivery. You do this by more thought and more consideration to the speed of your speech, such as whether you are speaking loudly or softly. Actually the change of pitch and change of pace can hold an audience for you if they become a little restless. At times an audience may have heard a number of speeches before your time on the program. Sometimes it takes more skill to hold onto your audience than it does if you are the only speaker, so you must learn to focus your entire attention on the audience, watching for those mood changes.

As you become more and more skilled in speaking, you will recognize that audiences send out "vibes." If you are alert to this and can change accordingly, you never lose them. If your speech is not going very well, you get bad vibes. This is a form of stare instead of a responsive expression from your audience. Make no mistake about it—no one will have to point it out to you—you'll see it. You must be alert to it and be prepared to change if necessary so that you can get back in control again. The skillful speaker watches for this mood change, this change of vibes, and is constantly alert and delivers accordingly.

Eye Contact

Keeping eye contact is one of the most valuable techniques in studying audience mood and in understanding their vibes. Whatever you do, look in all areas of the audience. Don't just look to one side, don't just look down front and never look deep into the audience. Don't look over the front rows and appear to be looking constantly at the back rows. Change your eye contact from time to time to all over the room. Audiences like to feel you are talking directly to them individually. Individuals want to be recognized by the speaker looking directly their way occasionally. Speakers who fail, who do not effectively deliver their speeches, are those who have not learned to work with the audience, to focus on the audience, and to keep good eye contact.

It's possible that as you go along you will have an occasion to feel as if your speech isn't going too well. Here is where you practice the skill of looking at one friendly person until you get over being flustered and get your bearings again. Once you get back into a smooth tempo and your speech is being received as you want it to be, you can once again get eye contact all over the room.

Be careful that you don't change your eye contact too frequently. This tends to make you appear shifty-eyed and not able to look at a person or group squarely. Let your eyes roam over the audience slowly but regularly. Occasionally look down the middle of the audience for a few moments and then go back to moving your eye contact around the room, down front, to the back and to each side. You'll find that this will help you to remain focused on the audience.

Another thing to watch out for is to not change eye contact too quickly. This gives the appearance of someone watching a tennis match. It appears mechanical and insincere. Move your eyes around the audience regularly, frequently but carefully, so that it will have a proper effect on the audience. This, more than any other one thing, will help you maintain that power of audience control! Look at all of your audience and all of your audience will look at you.

Give It Punch

Use words that have punch. Select carefully the words you want to use in each and every passage of your speech. I am talking about delivery in this book, but I am also, to some extent, talking about preparation. If you have a good vocabulary and if you think on your feet, as skillful speakers do, then you will come up with the right words. Your words will have punch, they will have fire, they will have a dramatic effect on the audience because they fit what you are saying and give that added punch.

Be sure to give your words some color, but not off-color. This means words that are descriptive, words that come to life for you and the audience. Give your words color along with punch!

Use simple words. The most famous speeches of all times are speeches that were delivered with complete simplicity. This is not to the point of talking down to the audience but simply using everyday language that fits you and fits your audience. Over and over and over you will learn that simplicity is the most effective way of all for good communications.

But by all means, occasionally use some so-called ten-dollar words. These ten-dollar words let your audience know that you are a learned person, that you are an educated person, that you have more than just a street vocabulary. Don't overdo it because if there are people in the audience not familiar with some of these words or terminology, you will leave them behind. While they think about what you've just said, they miss what you say as you continue, and you lose control.

Watch out for repetition. It becomes quite easy to have a few pet words that you use over and over in a speech. Learn to say the same thing in different words so that repetition will not be noticed. You don't want the audience to begin to count the times you use a particular word or phrase.

In giving your speech punch, you must learn to put emphasis on certain words. Again, go back to words with punch and color. Some words are easier to emphasize than others. Emphasis in delivery of a speech is *timing*, and timing is the factor that makes a speaker successful. The ability to use colorful words with punch and give them real emphasis in the proper place is essential. So, it behooves you to be thinking constantly about words. Speakers are "word-smiths;" you need to think constantly of how to make your words come alive with real meaning. It makes no difference if you are speaking from a key-word outline, from a typed outline, or from a full manuscript. You can give it punch not only in the preparation, but in the actual delivery. Remember, speech without punch is very tiring to listen to.

Paint Word Pictures

If the audience is to visualize what you are saying, you must first visualize your ideas. When you learn to visualize ideas, then you can put these ideas into words that paint word pictures. This will help you deliver forcefully and maintain *control* and *interest*.

Once you learn to visualize your ideas, then the next step is to picture your ideas in words. When you learn to picture your ideas in this way, then you can paint word pictures for your audience as you go. You've often heard the compliment paid some speakers that they are great story-tellers. Well, they are great storytellers because they tell stories in such a way that the audience can actually visualize what they are saying. This keeps them involved and listening. This is audience control!

If you relate passages that call for action or describe action, be animated. Gestures are covered in a later chapter but this simply means that you must learn to breathe life into your speech by being animated, and you cannot be animated about your speech if you don't feel it.

Mannerisms

First and foremost, unless you are using a hand micro-phone and walking around the room, *stand still*. A speaker at a big sales rally meeting, in which there is a highly motivated audience and is covering subjects that have a tendency to inspire motivation, may like to work with a hand mike and move around a bit as he or she delivers. When you move around it does help keep the audience's attention but you still have to deliver a good message. Simply moving around with a hand mike and no message isn't enough. But if you are standing behind the podium, stand still. Don't keep moving around and getting your voice away from the mike; stand still to deliver your talk.

Stand erect. A speaker not standing erect, one who

droops or hunches over, certainly has no positive effect on an audience. Deliver in a positive way. You simply cannot do this if you are not standing erect.

Let your tie alone. Leave your necktie alone! Occasionally you will see speakers who pull their tie up or straighten it several times during their talk. Any time this type of action is taken by a speaker, it has a tendency to draw attention from what he is saying and to have the audience thinking, "I wish he could get that necktie straightened. I wonder if he likes the way it is now? I wonder if he's going to change it again?" These negative thoughts can creep into your delivery if you are not careful. Fix your tie right before you begin your speech and it shouldn't be any problem from then on. This nervous habit is even easier to get into if you are wearing a bow tie, such as in a black tie situation. Get the proper tie and quit working at it as you try to deliver a speech. It is very distracting.

Glasses on or glasses off. The same goes for glasses! Recently I attended a roast and one of the roasters, a very famous person, who just a few years ago was a household name across America, a highly educated person and a very experienced and knowledgeable person, during his entire roast presentation, kept taking his glasses off. It seems as if he took his glasses off when he started a sentence and put them back on when he ended it. Someone sitting at my table said, "I wonder if he's ever going to get through changing those glasses?" Make up your mind either to wear glasses and leave them on, or take them off. This has become a very unpopular action by some speakers and has a bad effect on their delivery.

Don't draw attention to time. Such things as wearing a watch with a chain can be bad for it may be hard to keep your hands off the watch chain. If you must look at your watch, take it out midway through the speech or near the end for timing purposes, then keep your hands off of it from then on.

Don't even look at your watch if you can possibly avoid it. If you're lucky, there will be a clock somewhere on the wall in the meeting room or the auditorium. If not, and you are quite concerned about finishing on time or if you've been asked to cut a little bit in order to get the program back on schedule, then take your watch off or out of your pocket and lay it on the podium. If you are speaking away from the podium, such as with a hand mike, you will want to learn to glance at your watch quickly without drawing the attention of the audience to the time. Otherwise, they will begin to look at their watches and begin to think about things other than the message you are delivering.

Rocking back and forth. Don't rock back and forth. This has a tendency to irritate an audience. It may have a tendency to put them to sleep!

Rocking side to side. Don't rock side to side. In one of my speech classes I had a young fellow who was somewhat nervous, as most people are when they first begin to study speech delivery. He would get into his talk and begin to do what appeared to be something like a rhumba step. It was a little box step and he just went round and round with it. As he became more comfortable with things I got him to quit this little box step and his delivery greatly improved.

Unbutton and button. You occasionally see speakers who are constantly buttoning and unbuttoning their coats or vests. They have a tendency to button and unbutton and keep on doing this during their talk. Obviously it's an outlet for nerves but it has a tendency to distract the audience. Nothing should be done on stage or in a speaking situation that in any way could possibly distract those people and have them watching more than listening.

Coat lapel. Another irritating habit is constantly putting your hand on your coat lapel. Speakers will grip their coat lapel and hold it up there for the longest time, finally letting it down, but before you know it, their hand is back up there again gripping that coat lapel. This is just another one of those nervous, irritating habits that has a tendency to distract from your talk.

Handkerchief. Let your pocket handkerchief alone, not only the handkerchief in your outside coat pocket. You sometimes actually see speakers reaching into their hip pocket to get a pocket handkerchief out. Now if you need it to wipe your brow, if it's a hot room and you are perspiring, that's something else; but keep in mind that every time you do something like that, you have a danger of leading the audience into the same act. They become more aware of heat and the uncomfortable aspects of the room. So let the hand-kerchief alone. Certainly don't use it as a toy as you deliver your talk.

Hair. Don't keep pushing your hair back. If you comb your hair well before you go on stage, it should stay in place. If a lock or two falls down onto your forehead, it's not nearly as distracting as to keep pulling away at it and pushing back on it—just another thing that has a bad effect on the audience.

Squint. Don't squint at the audience. Look at them wide-eyed. Squinting has a tendency to make your facial expression different than you want it to be. So learn not to squint as you deliver your talk.

Pen or pencil. Let your pen and pencil alone. Occasionally you'll see a speaker who will take his or her pen out only to put it back in his or her pocket and take it out again. This is an irritating distraction.

Rattling change. One of the most common and most irritating of habits, particularly for the small audience, is to be rattling change in your pocket.

Finger. Don't wave your finger at an audience. I will talk more about this in the section on gestures. Use your *hands* to point, not your fingers. People don't like speakers who point at them.

Drinking water. Last but not least, if at all possible, get all the way through your speech without drinking water. There are exceptions of course. If you have been taking cold medicine or some medication and you have a dry throat, nothing can be done about it except to ease it with water; that cannot be helped. After all you don't cancel a speech because of a slight cold. You have to deliver! However, using the glass of water gets the mind of the audience on their need for water, on *their* thirst, and it tends to detract from your delivery. Try your best to go without water.

If it's a long program and you must have water, then by all means do it quickly, without fanfare. You can sip from your glass during a break in the talk, a transition point, or maybe during a little laughter. If you feel that you might need water, check and be sure some is available so you will have it when you need it and won't have to look all over the room to find it.

All of the nervous mannerisms can be eliminated if you will just direct that energy into putting more feeling into your words!

A Good Speaking Voice

Here are nine essentials for a good speaking voice. These will help you learn what is expected for an effective delivery:

1. A good average speed of delivery
2. Distinct pronunciation
3. Accurate pronunciation
4. Conversational inflection
5. Earnestness and sincerity
6. Pitch variation—freedom of monotone
7. Selective emphasis of key words
8. Ability to make pauses; punctuate
9. Freedom from word whiskers; ah, er, uh

There is no way to cover these points on good speaking voice without thinking of Dave Yoho, CPAE, one of America's great platform speakers. Dave was born with a speech impediment. Despite this speech handicap, he got into selling and became a top producer in every selling assignment he has ever had. After a great success in selling, he became a sales trainer and quickly became nationally famous. This, of course, led into many other types of speaking engagements and even though he continues as Chief Executive for his various enterprises, he is in great demand as the featured speaker. He is articulate; he is dramatic; he is eloquent! He has the power to control his audiences and inspire them to reach for new heights. A good speaking voice is important, and Dave Yoho has proven that this skill can be attained.

Video Taping

Some speakers take the opportunity to study themselves on video tape. This is probably the most effective way to improve your speech delivery. Obviously it is not as beneficial as an actual experience before a live audience, and taping yourself before a live audience is better still, for then you really see what you look like to the audience.

Another good way to study your delivery is to have a friend in the audience who will tell you what he or she observes as you deliver your speech, and let you know if you have any of the irritating mannerisms discussed previously. Be sure you get someone who will tell you the truth and not just tell you what he or she thinks you would like to hear.

Rising Inflection

Rising inflection means to bring your voice from a lower pitch to a higher pitch. Here are some points that describe what occurs when a rising inflection is used:

1. A rising inflection asks a question.
2. A rising inflection expresses indecision.
3. A rising inflection indicates hesitation.
4. A rising inflection suggests suspense.
5. A rising inflection implies doubt.
6. A rising inflection suggests timidity.

Falling Inflection

This brings your voice from a higher pitch to a lower pitch, which is needed sometimes. This is a forceful way to use certain passages in your speech. The lower pitch voice is called the voice of an executive and you want to sound this way in certain parts of your speech. Here's what falling inflection denotes:

1. Determination
2. Confidence
3. Finality (this often makes it usable at the end of a speech)
4. An answer to a question
5. Firmness
6. Decisiveness
7. Dogmatism

Habitual rising inflection denotes a lack of confidence, while a lower inflection denotes authority and confidence. These can be used in various ways in your speech delivery.

Rules of Basic Speaking

Effective speech is not for exhibition but rather for communication. Effective speech has for its ultimate end the winning of response. In other words, get that audience to do what you want them to do or to feel as you want them to feel.

The effective speaker uses the techniques of speech in order to bring attention to a peak, bearing on the response he or she seeks. Any technique of speech that draws undue attention to itself defeats its purpose. Crudeness, awkwardness, and eccentricity draw attention to themselves and therefore defeat your purpose. Virtuosity, pomposity, or grandiloquence, which attract attention, is artless.

Effective speech, when it's all said and done, is disarming in its apparent spontaneity, its simplicity, its ease. An able speaker is a person with a good emotional state and good attitude toward him or herself and toward his or her audience. Impressions of a speaker are derived from actions of which the audience is often unaware.

Visualize success—a positive approach. The effective professional speaker has learned to actually visualize him or herself before a particular audience and actually sees him or herself delivering a meaningful speech. He or she can actually visualize that audience with warm responsive faces accepting what is said as he or she goes along from point to point. Obviously this is optimism. This is a positive outlook on the occasion. This is exercising audience control!

Be yourself—absolutely! Never try to be anyone else. I like the way Bill Gove, CPAE, founding president of NSA says it,

> Today I have a responsibility to you, the audience as a speaker, to stay on time and share with you feelings that I've had. I have a responsibility to stay within the framework of the meeting. I have a responsibility to you, to be at my very best. You can't have me any better than that. You might have someone else better but you can't have Bill Gove any better than his best. That's my responsibility to you, the audience—but I will not accept any responsibility for your behavior toward me. Hope you like me—but if you don't—(that's) not my problem!

Bill Gove is one of the all-time greats as a platform speaker. He has often been referred to as a "speaker's speaker" by other professionals. If being yourself is good enough for Bill Gove, it's good enough for all of us. We all need to work on being an improved self!

*****

For example, let me tell you about. . . .

7

Discovering the Art
of Telling Stories

Make your anecdotes pay off

Anecdotes are stories, accounts of incidents, told in narrative form. They may be mythical, they may be true. Using anecdotes in a speech breathes more life into the speech than any other technique that can be used. Good writing always includes examples. The best speeches are filled with anecdotes . . . good stories told well to support the point that has just been made. Usually they are used after a point that is considered one of the main parts of the speech has been made. The anecdote will follow. Sometimes the anecdote can be used as a transition point.

Never Read the Anecdote

This means that the anecdotes, case histories, and examples must be memorized—not memorized word for word, but at least the story line, so that as the speech progresses anecdotes may be used to drive home a point, perhaps when not really planned into the speech. This book is about delivery, and while most anecdotes are planned, or should be planned, the accomplished speaker has a number of anecdotes that come to mind while delivering a speech.

It's entirely possible that you may plan to use one or more anecdotes during the talk and for one reason or another, during the talk, change direction and use an anecdote that comes to mind or that seems to fit the occasion better. This could be brought on by something that has been said previously in the program. It could be a somewhat different audience makeup than you anticipated. It could be that some current event prompts a change in your speech delivery. The story must be memorized, so that under no circumstances are these stories, incidents, examples, or case histories read; they should be *told*. Reading an anecdote is probably the worst thing that could be done in the delivery of a speech.

Must Be Interesting

Here is a story that, if told well, should be of interest to all in the audience. The person it is told about and what takes place will probably interest any audience.

> Back in the 30's a young woman walked into a book agent's office in New York City with a manuscript of over 1,000 pages in her hands. The book agent whistled when she laid it on his desk and said, "It's too long. Who in the world is going to wade through all of that? Can you shorten it?"
>
> "I suppose I could," the woman replied disconsolately.
>
> "I presume this is your first novel," the book agent said.
>
> She answered, "Yes, it is."
>
> The book agent asked, "Have you ever published anything before?"
>
> "No."
>
> "What is the story about?"
>
> "A young woman living in the South during the Civil War."
>
> "Too bad you didn't locate it in the West; westerns are very popular right now. What do you call your book?"

"Gone with the Wind."

"Publishers won't touch it. It's too big a risk. A book by an unknown would have to be another American Tragedy to make a profit. Publishers have economic problems that young writers do not understand. They could publish three books for the price that it would take to publish yours . . . I'll give you the name of a friend of mine who may handle it for you. He has sold a few historical novels, but first I'd strongly recommend that you chop it in half . . . it's too long."

You can see that this is an interesting story that unfolds in an interesting way. The character, of course, is Margaret Mitchell. The book agent is unknown. This is a true incident, a story told over and over because of the phenomenal success of the book, Gone with the Wind, which was later made into a motion picture. It made publishing history as well as motion picture history. This truly is an interesting anecdote and one that shouldn't miss any audience. You could easily use this anecdote to support the points you may want to make on dedication, perseverance, or simply faith in one's ability.

Should Be Short

Here is a short anecdote that is as up to date as today:

A small boy came home from school with the news that he was second in his class. Top place, he said, was held by a girl.

"Surely, Jack," said the father, "you're not going to be beaten by a mere girl"?

"Well, you see, Dad," explained Jack, "girls are not nearly as mere as they used to be."

This would be an interesting and short anecdote to tell to a group in which you believe there are a number of career women. This type of story points out the fact that times are changing . . . women are doing things they didn't used to do and you are comfortable with this thought. It would help you to prove to the audience that when you speak to them along the lines of career objectives, that you sincerely feel women have the right to step forward and to make progress. It is up to you to convince the audience that you feel comfortable with the role women play today.

Here's another short anecdote with actual names not given. It supports the point that the modern businessperson has to advertise and use all of the modern marketing tools in order to reach great success.

> A local merchant prided himself on not ever having to advertise. Regardless of what happened in his trade area, he wanted to get by without spending money on advertising, promotion, or other modern techniques of marketing. Finally, though, he did have to advertise, because as times changed, he failed to keep up with all of his competitors in the area, who began to advertise and promote. His first step into advertising was to stick a sign on his door that read, "Bankruptcy Sale—See the Sheriff."

This, of course, means that he failed in business because he would not advertise, would not use the modern techniques. A good point to use in describing and supporting your forceful statement about the need for up-to-date marketing techniques.

Here's another example of a short anecdote that may be used:

> "Why take chances," says the farmer. A backwoods farmer, sitting on the steps of a tumble-down shack, was approached by a stranger who stopped for a drink of water.
>
> "How's your wheat coming along?" asked the stranger.
>
> "Didn't plant none."
>
> "Really, I thought this was good wheat country."
>
> "Afraid it would rain."

> "Well, how is your corn crop?"
>
> "Ain't got none. Afraid of corn blight."
>
> The stranger, confused but persevering continued, "Well, how are your potatoes?"
>
> "Didn't plant no potatoes either . . . afraid of potato bugs."
>
> "For Pete's sake, man," the stranger asked, "What did you plant?"
>
> "Nothing," said the farmer, "I just played it safe."

This is a good example to point out that life itself is a risk, that no one ever succeeded in anything good that didn't involve a risk or a gamble. The whole system, and this includes farming, is built around a certain risk factor that those who succeed must take chances. This would support the point that you might tell the audience: don't be afraid to make progress by taking a chance. This certainly beats sitting back and doing nothing.

Here's another example of a short anecdote that you may want to use to support the fact that everyone makes mistakes in business and in living.

> A paratrooper in Ft. Benning, Georgia, where they train paratroopers, asked his top sergeant, "Sarge, how many jumps do I have to complete to graduate?"
>
> "All of them . . . all of them," replied the top sergeant.

You could add to it by saying, "We all make mistakes; we're not like the paratrooper who isn't allowed any mistakes in order to graduate." This is another example of a short anecdote or incident that may be used to support that type of point.

Humorous Anecdotes

Here is an anecdote that can be used to tell an audience that it's good to be meeting with a group who is all for the same thing and it is especially suitable for early in your talk.

> The story is told that years ago the Lord of
> Coventry raised the taxes so high in Coventry that
> the little people suffered. His beautiful wife, Lady
> Godiva, was more compassionate, shall we say,
> than the Lord. She went to him and told him that if
> he would lower the taxes she would ride through
> the streets of Coventry without any clothes on,
> seated on a white horse. The Lord of Coventry did
> reduce the taxes, and he was anxious to see if Lady
> Godiva would live up to her part of the bargain.
> She did, and on one beautiful sunny morning rode
> through the streets of Coventry on a beautiful white
> horse, with no clothes on. She rode sidesaddle that
> morning, and half the people in town were shout-
> ing, "Hooray for our side."

This story is particularly good when addressing an audience
who are all for the same thing. It could be a professional
group such as doctors, lawyers, accountants, or managers,
who meet together regularly as a group for the betterment of
their profession. It could be for a corporate group in their
annual meeting in which you could acknowledge their desire to improve their company in every way possible. It is
ideal for a sales meeting in which you can point out that,
unlike the people of Coventry, they are all for greater sales,
greater share of market, etc. You could end this particular
passage by saying it's great to be with a group who is all for
the same thing.

Here's another example of a humorous anecdote that
may be used in various ways and was probably used in this
case to get a certain amount of humility after an introduction.

> John McKay, coach of the Tampa Bay Buc-
> caneers, began a luncheon talk on a note of
> appreciation. "It's nice of you to have me when
> we're two and ten. I'm lucky to even get invited
> home to dinner."

This points out something that most audiences would know,
particularly during football season, that the Tampa Bay Buc-

caneers had a miserable two or three seasons of start-up football. They were barely able to stay on the field. This was John McKay's humorous way of acknowledging an introduction at that time. You, the speaker, use this early in a talk as you acknowledge your introduction. This is about someone who is somewhat in the news and readily identifiable by your audience.

Here's another example of a very short and humorous statement that may be considered a form of anecdote even though it is a one-liner.

> *The fortune tellers convention in Atlanta was recently postponed because of unforseen circumstances.*

This says it all. You could support a point that nothing is definite but death and taxes and this could easily support your point that there are no certainties, that you have to keep struggling all the time to make good things happen. There's no such thing as a free lunch.

Here's another humorous anecdote somewhat related to sports that would be particularly good for a golfing group.

> *A fellow was convicted of murder and thrown into prison. His cellmate asked, "What brings you here?"*
>
> *The newcomer said, "I killed my wife. She kept bugging me because I was always out on the golf course and was never home. Every time I came back from a game she was on my back. One day after a particularly lousy round of golf she started in on me. I went out of my mind and conked her on the head with a golf club."*
>
> *"What club did you use?" the cellmate asked.*
>
> *"A seven iron."*
>
> *"How many strokes did it take?"*
>
> *"Two."*
>
> *"How come it took you two strokes?" his cellmate asked.*
>
> *The fellow replied, "I looked up!"*

All golfers know it's a cardinal sin in golf to look up when you swing the golf club. This is a humorous way of telling the audience how important golf is to some people, or how some people take their golf so seriously that it actually will lead to murder. Somewhat exaggerated, yes, but a good anecdote.

Here's another short and quick anecdote that tells it all.

> A middle-aged Italian couple sat in the front row of their son's graduation from Purdue University. As the president of the university began to speak, the woman nudged her husband and asked, "What did he say?"
>
> "Who?" asked the father.
>
> "The beeg fella in blacka robe—what did he say?"
>
> Her husband replied, "He say school is out."

Now you see that this is a quick way of using a little anecdote to liven up your speech and to make a point where this type of story would fit.

Your Stories Must Be Supportive

I used this anecdote in Chapter 3. It has been used by several speakers and I first heard it used by the late Bill Alexander, the famous minister and public speaker of Oklahoma City. I use it to support the point that wives really are a great deal of help to husbands who are businessmen, professionals, or who are trying to carve out their own career in this world. Stating that wives are a great deal of help to their husbands, and to break up the serious thoughts for a few moments, I say:

> Of course there are exceptions. For example, just the other day I was attending the dedication of a huge new building out in Houston, Texas, and I was standing next to a fellow who remarked, "my wife made a millionaire out of me." He said it in

such a way that I was prompted to ask, "What were you before?" He replied, "A multi-millionaire."

This points out how you can have a little play on words and also points out the fact that there are exceptions to every rule. The wives laugh as hard at this line as the husbands do. So it isn't new, it still works, because when it's told properly it helps to make your point and that's what anecdotes are all about.

Here's another anecdote that I use from time to time that's a true story and has to do with good sales management and time planning.

A sales manager friend of mine out in the Midwest is an absolute nut about time planning. He had a veteran salesperson retire and a young rookie replaced him. Now this particular sales manager drills over and over about time planning, especially to his newly assigned salespeople.

He had this new salesperson spend three days out in the mill to learn something about production, quality control, etc., then the fourth day in the office with the credit manager (sometimes referred to as the sales prevention department), then the last day with him. This is when he really drove home his points about time planning.

With this particular new salesperson he must have gotten his message over because after he assigned him to his new territory several states away from home office, he received a call from a longtime customer and friend. This friend told him that he had a fine young man representing the company but maybe he had better slow him down a bit. The friend said the young salesperson had been in to see him the day before and opened his interview by saying, "If you will just buy now, you can save yourself a dull 20-minute sales presentation."

This is an excellent anecdote to use with any business group, especially where there are sales managers or salespeople in the audience. This is not a long story but I still like to break it up with the aside about credit managers (sometimes referred to as the sales prevention department). This aside slipped into this passage unplanned one time and it got such a good laugh that I continued to work it into the story.

I end by saying to the audience, "That may be a little too fast."

Here's another anecdote, case history, example—whatever you prefer to call it—and it's used when I talk along the lines of enthusiasm. First, I mention that when I talk about enthusiasm I think of people like Pete Rose of the Philadelphia Phillies, who runs to first base even when he gets a base on balls. Now he is instantly recognized and nearly everyone know him as Charlie Hustle.

Then I go into this story about the sales manager in the retail situation who had a young fellow working for him that he thought had all of the requirements for successful selling, but who wasn't succeeding. He watched him for a few days and decided that this young fellow just wasn't enthusiastic, so he called him over one afternoon and said,

> "I want you to turn over a new leaf tomorrow. I think you've got everything going for you, but you're just not breathing any life into your sales contacts. You're simply not enthusiastic. Now in the morning when the clock goes off, I want you to hit the deck running, right through your shower and shave, and come on down here really turned on."
>
> The very next morning the young fellow was two hours late. The sales manager said, "I thought this was a new day. I thought you were going to turn over a new page and come in here excited."
>
> The young fellow spoke up, "Sure, I did everything you told me to. The clock went off, I hit the deck fast, went through my shower and shave, went downstairs, kissed my wife enthusiastically . . . and that's why I'm two hours late."

You can see this supports your heavy thoughts . . . your heavy statements about enthusiasm and the need for it by lightening up the message just a little bit. And then you could say, "don't get overenthusiastic."

Here's another humorous anecdote used to tell about reassuring the customer, the prospect, the client, or anyone you're trying to sell, lead, or persuade. It can be used as a key note for conventions, or professional groups such as a sales and marketing meeting.

> *A young fellow walked through a used car lot and spotted the salesman he thought had sold him a car the week before. He asked, "Sir, aren't you the gentleman that sold me that car last week?"*
>
> *The salesman looked out to the curb, saw the car, and said, "Yes, I believe I am."*
>
> *The young fellow said, "Sell me again, I'm getting discouraged."*

You see, it's a quick, short way of supporting the point that you have to reassure even your established customers sometimes.

Another quick example of a short and humorous thought that is used to support the fact that this is a time of cultural change is this:

> *A college president was asked, "Doesn't it bother you that your department heads continue to use the same examination questions over and over?"*
>
> *The college president answered, "No, not really. You see, we keep changing the answers."*

You've reminded your audience that they live in constant change and they have to pay attention to be sure that they will be able to keep up. Here's another humorous, short incident that happens to be a true story.

> *A man walked up to a Coca-Cola vending machine in Charlotte, North Carolina, and put his*

*money in the machine, but the Coca-Cola didn't
come out and neither did the money. He became
highly frustrated. He stepped back, took out a gun,
and shot the vending machine six times and was
reloading to get off another shot when the police
got there.*

This happens to be true. It was reported in the Charlotte
News and Observer, talking about the frustrations of living,
the frustration of present day life.

I usually follow up by saying, "Of course *we'll* never
reach that height of frustration." Then, "Ladies, for you the
height of frustration would be if your husband and Burt
Reynolds were fighting over you . . . and your husband was
winning."

When you are speaking in story form to your audience
you may have a tendency to continue oratory that sometimes
creeps into your delivery because of the strong points you've
made. This gives you an opportunity to relax a little yourself,
as well as relax your audience, even though it's not necessarily humorous anecdotes. It will help you to change the pace
of your program.

Here's a sports anecdote that's told in story form:

*The late Danny Murtaugh, when manager of
the Pittsburgh Pirates, heard so many fantastic accounts of a young man pitching for an American
Legion team in South Carolina, that he went personally to investigate. He contacted the fellow one
afternoon as he was warming up to pitch a game.
Murtaugh said, "Let me see your fast ball." It was a
dandy. "Now let me see your slider." It, too, was
something to behold. "Now let me see your move to
first," meaning his pitch to first to hold the runner
on base.*

"My what?"

*"Your move to first. Show me how you keep a
runner close to the bag when he's on first."*

The young man said solemnly, "Mr. Mur-

taugh, when I'm pitching, nobody ever gets on first!"

It has everything. It has names, it has dialogue. It has humor.

Here's another example of a good story told and delivered by the speaker in story form.

> *Winston Churchill was scheduled to make a radio broadcast one afternoon. He hailed a cab, saying, "Take me to the BBC Studios."*
>
> *"Sorry, sir. You'll have to take another cab. I can't go that far."*
>
> *The former Prime Minister was rather surprised and asked why.*
>
> *"Mr. Churchill is broadcasting," replied the driver, "and I want to get home and tune in."*
>
> *Churchill pulled out a pound note. The driver took one look at the money and said, "Hop in, the hell with Mr. Churchill."*

This also has everything. It has dialogue. It has an instantly recognized name. It has an unusual twist at the end, which always helps a story to be a little better. All of these are good for grabbing attention.

Here's another anecdote told in story form that helps to make a point when you think of possible career direction or the uncertainties of living.

> *"Someone helped me when I was a kid," says Sugar Ray Robinson. "My mother worked in the laundry and I ran around the streets looking for trouble. I got into a crap game one day outside the church. The cops came along and everyone started to run. I stayed behind to pick up the money.*
>
> *"But while the cops were chasing the other kids, the minister came out of the church and caught me. He led me downstairs to the gym. There was a basketball court and a punching bag. The bag intrigued me and if it weren't for this crazy*

> *chain of events, God knows what would have happened to me."*

Now, many people know that Sugar Ray Robinson was a renowned prize fighter and world champion, one of the most popular fighters of all time, respected and admired by the sports world at large, as well as his fans.

Here's another example of talking about success that could be used in a motivational, inspirational type of talk or to an employee.

Joe Girard, well-known author of *How to Sell Anything to Anybody* writes:

> *The elevator to success is out of order. You'll have to use the stairs . . . one step at a time.*

This is short, quick and to the point, and it helps to drive home the idea that there are no short cuts to success at anything.

In his famous film, "The Strangest Secret," Earl Nightingale says:

> *There's nothing particularly wrong with watching television all the time . . . except that the person doing so is watching other people who are earning an excellent income in the pursuit of their careers . . . while he doesn't make a nickel. And he gets the only two things you can get from watching on that type of a schedule . . . he gets red eyes and a hollow head.*

That tells it all. It means you have to give up some of your leisure time, some of your fun time, if you want to get a bigger bite out of life, if you want to succeed in a big way. You have to decide what you want, what you'll give up to get it and then you have to go about getting it done and sacrifice some of your fun things.

Speaking of confidence in a speech could be supported by this little statement or account of someone instantly recognizable.

Speaking of confidence reminds me of the late Dizzy Dean, who was one of the foremost national figures as far as self-confidence is concerned. He was a great baseball pitcher, a big winner, and he went on to become world famous as a telecaster in baseball. Dizzy Dean, known for his confidence, used to make this statement. It's an all-meaning thought, a profound thought: "It ain't braggin' if you can do it."

You can see that this will support any comment you may be making on building faith, building confidence, or positive thinking.

The more famous a person is, the easier it is to tell a story about him or her, because you have no fear that the audience doesn't know exactly who you're talking about, and that in fact, they visualize that person as you tell your story. Quite a few, of course, are told about the chief executive officer of the United States, the president. Here's one told about Woodrow Wilson, before he took office, that points out how humility can be used.

Just after Woodrow Wilson was elected President of the United States he went to visit his elderly and almost deaf Aunt Jane. She asked him what he had been doing, and he shouted, "I've been elected President."

"President of what?"

"President of the United States."

"Don't be silly," Aunt Jane said, ending the conversation.

Here's another example of the President of the United States being humbled in an unusual way.

When LBJ was President he went to church one Sunday morning accompanied by the Secret Service and motorcycle police. After the service he was approached by a small boy who asked him, "Are you the guy who came with the police?"

LBJ replied, "Yes, sonny, I am."
"Well, you'd better duck out the back door,"
the lad said, "they're still out there waiting for
you."

This is another good example, which you may want to
put it into your own words, or use the actual quotations as
they were reported.

Living Examples

There are a number of good examples of how you can
give biographical facts to build up a story, particularly when
it's someone who has become famous but started with rather
modest beginnings. Here's a case history that I use quite
often in talking about the will to win and burning desire.

W. Clement Stone, as a young boy, was put out
on the streets of Chicago's tough southside to sell
newspapers. The older bigger boys beat him up and
ran him off the best corners. W. Clement Stone
didn't get discouraged. He had to make good, he
had to succeed, he had to get newspapers sold. He
found a restaurant the other boys didn't know
about and every afternoon he went in and sold out
his newspapers.

Today, W. Clement Stone is one of the wealth-
iest men in North America. He is principal owner
of Combined Insurance Corporation of America.
He does a lot to inspire and encourage young
people, and people of all ages, to make the most out
of their opportunities. He participates in positive
mental attitude clinics and big mass meetings. He
is a success story and he is willing to share his
thoughts, his approach to life, and his success with
others. He is so wealthy that he gives tremendously
large amounts of money to both political parties in
order to show his faith in the system. W. Clement

Stone is truly a success story as it relates to starting with humble beginnings and reaching a high level.

This is a good example that can be used in trying to encourage people not to give up, to have faith, to keep working, and to have that positive mental approach to life and to living.

Here's another example that is used somewhat along the same lines. It may also be used to support your statement to the group that you're never too old to want and to achieve success.

Colonel Sanders, at age 65, already on Social Security, founded with less than $500 one of the most fantastic food chains we will ever know. He changed your eating habits and mine to some extent. Colonel Sanders didn't give up. He had an idea, saw that he could make it work, and he put everything he had into it. The rest is business history.

Here's another good example, especially for women. It could be used to support an organization where there are a lot of career women, or to support a point that women now have opportunities they've never had before and it's up to them to make the most of these opportunities.

Mary Kay, who founded Mary Kay Cosmetics in 1963 after she retired, and which is now one of the most successful businesses of its kind ever ($250 million in retail sales in 1980), tells the women in her audience, usually at the beginning of the talk, "When God made the world, He looked down and said, 'That's good'—and then he made a man—and said, 'That's good—but I think I can do better'—so he made a woman! (Even an artist makes a rough draft first!)"

That, of course, supports the statement that you've been making in your primary message, that there are opportunities for women now like never before.

Self-Explanatory

In telling a story, giving a case history, or relating an incident, it's very important that you make the story you tell self-explanatory. Don't leave any doubt in the minds of the audience as to how it unfolds or what it means.

Here is a true story that I use from time to time in connection with affluence. I will normally get into it by saying that we're living in affluent times. I point out that the American people spend almost $2 billion a year on dog food and over $1 billion a year on dog clothes, and then I say:

> *I used to live next door to a very successful and highly attractive couple who were childless. They had no children but had a little puppy (about so high?) named Pixie. Pixie got all the love and affection that a child of theirs would have been given and I find nothing wrong with that.*
>
> *I was invited over one time for Chirstmas Eve. After cocktails, dinner, and a cigar, the hostess started bringing the gifts from under the tree to the small group of people who were there. Now I don't remember where the first two gifts went, but I shall never forget where gift number three went. It was to "Kirk" from "Pixie." Now, this was embarrassing. First of all it was the first time I've ever received a gift from a dog, and worst of all, I didn't have anything for Pixie."*

Now you can see that this is self-explanatory. It points out that here is a couple so wrapped up in their little pet, their little puppy Pixie, that they go to the trouble of wrapping the Christmas presents to their guests with Pixie's name on it. Now, it sounds ridiculous and I've told it over and over to audiences, but they always see the very humorous side of this. So, when you can tell an incident such as this that is true, it makes a lot of difference.

Here's another anecdote that I have used off and on for

quite some time. This true story has to do with supporting
the point of self-confidence.

A couple of years ago I was attending a convention out in Hot Springs, Arkansas. The convention ended on Saturday noon but the weather had
turned extremely bad and the ceiling had dropped
right down onto the field at the small airport. We
waited about two hours and finally our little plane
came in, a DC-3. We climbed aboard, took off, and
headed east for a change of planes in Memphis and
on to Atlanta.

Now, if you're not familiar with a DC-3,
they're very small planes. You don't see many of
them anymore, but they are the forerunners of the
big birds you see today. Big moneymaker, great
safety record, but very small.

As we started towards Memphis for our
change, this little plane had to stop to make—I call
it a whistle stop—in Pine Bluff, Arkansas. Just as
that little plane started down to approach the land-
ing in Pine Bluff, I looked out the window and
could hardly see the wingtip. Ladies and gentlemen, regardless of how much flying you do, and
this was an experienced group of air travelers
aboard the plane, you begin to worry just a little bit.
I looked around me on that plane, and I saw fear in
the faces of my fellow passengers, as I'm sure they
saw in mine.

About that time the intercom came on and a
strong masculine voice announced, "Ladies and
gentlemen, we'll be on the ground in Pine Bluff in
just a few minutes. It's raining, it's sleeting, and the
visibility is practically zero . . . so may I suggest
you be very careful driving home from the airport."

I go on to tell the audience that you can see that here was
a professional who had his fair share of self-confidence. He
had no fear that he could land that little old plane safely, and

you can see that he did. The important thing was that I looked around me on that plane, and where I saw fear before, I saw big broad grins on the faces of my fellow passengers, because they had been relieved, as I had, because the man up front had plenty of confidence.

Sports

Sports stories are good in practically any kind of meeting. The reason for this is that most Americans have one or more sports as their hobby, particularly those people who attend conventions or go to meetings. It's good to remind them of some of their sports heroes or some renowned figure in the world of sports. For the speaker it simplifies what he or she has to do because the sports figures are instantly recognizable. Here are several sports stories that I believe are self-explanatory. They are about people who are well-known and instantly recognizable, in most cases. They are stories that fit well as a follow up to a point of confidence, of fame, desire, or stickability.

The first one is an anecdote that I use often; it relates to having a positive attitude.

> The late Branch Rickey, called by many "the grand old man of baseball" because of his marvelous attitude, was asked by a St. Louis sportswriter on his 80th birthday, "How does it feel to be 80 years of age, Mr. Rickey?"
>
> Mr. Rickey replied quickly, with that marvelous attitude he had, "Son, it feels pretty darn wonderful when you consider the alternative."

Enough said; it's self-explanatory; it drives home the point that it's all a matter of how you look at things. It says that those people who make it big and who are highly successful are those people with good positive attitudes.

Here's another sports story of an instantly recognizable person. It, too, has a little bit of dialogue. Also, it has to do with positive living, the desire to win, dedication, and all of the things that go particularly well in inspiration, motivational-type talks.

> *The late Adolph Rupp, who was head basketball coach at the University of Kentucky over a period of 42 years with an 82 percent win record, a record that will probably never be broken, asked this question, "If winning isn't important, why keep score?" Now I don't think anyone in this meeting would deny the fact that Adolph Rupp did have the ability to win. He had the winning attitude and instilled it in the minds of his players because it was important to him.*

You can see this one short, simple sentence, when properly placed, tells it all and helps you to drive home your point that winning is important and that important people feel that way.

Here is a short one-liner in connection with winning.

> *Vince Lombardi, who became immortal as head coach of the Green Bay Packers, made this statement over and over again to his players, instilling in their minds the desire to win. "Winning is not the most important thing, it's the only thing."*

Here's another short one-liner that gives support to the importance of winning, the importance of desire, and the importance of dedication.

> *Bear Bryant, one of the winningest football coaches of all time, made this statement in one of his talks, "Show me 11 poor losers on a football team, and I'll show you a winning football team."*

Those statements may be used to support your beliefs. They can be used with feeling and a bit of emotion if you think that is the way you're supposed to feel as you cover this kind of material.

Here's another example of a sports story that has been

used by several speakers. It always makes a point because it supports the belief that you must have desire to really want to be a winner.

> Pete Gray . . . when I think of Pete Gray, I think of a burning desire in a human being. From the time Pete Gray was a young fellow, about Boy Scout age, he began to have a desire, a burning desire, to play baseball in Yankee Stadium. He finally made it with the old St. Louis Browns. Now you won't find Pete Gray in the Hall of Fame, but he is mentioned in the baseball record books and known by all real baseball fans. Pete Gray made his desire come true but Pete Gray made it all the way to Yankee Stadium with just one arm. (I usually follow it up by saying, "When I think of that kind of drive, that kind of self-confidence, I'm reminded of what a sissy I've been to let little things throw me.")

This is really a motivation-type of anecdote, and it's told with real feeling because this is what you're trying to drive home, the point that real feeling is involved.

Here's another sports story that I use and it happens to be true, as most of these are, and well documented, although not about a very famous person—not a Branch Rickey, Bear Bryant, Vince Lombardi, or Adolph Rupp reputation.

> I was in high school with a boy who made All-American High School Half-Back back in the days of one platoon football. Now think of that; he was one of the 11 best high school players in the United States. He went on to the University of Alabama, in the days when they played in the Rose Bowl. Charlie Boswell was a star player for the University of Alabama and then he went off to WWII. In a tank in Italy he came out of a bombing . . . stone blind.
>
> Charlie Boswell came home and, after a series of operations and hospital stays, he finally learned that he would be blind forever. Charlie Boswell

had lost his sight but he hadn't lost his spirit. He
had a strong body and a strong mind and he
wanted to use them, so he took up golf. He had
never played golf before. Now if you can picture a
blind golfer, shooting golf in the low 80's, then you
can really relate to a person having a burning desire and wanting to use what was left of his God-
given talents even though he had one of life's most
trying handicaps. He became the nation's No. 1
blind golfer year after year. To play golf blind
someone has to rattle the cup when you get on the
green. Someone has to stand and tell you when you
tee off the conditions of the fairway, whether it had
a dog leg or hook in it. Just imagine playing this
way and shooting in the low 80's! When I think of
that I think of a burning desire.

Here's another sports figure most of us are familiar with,
Monty Stratton.

Monty Stratton was injured on a hunting trip
in the off season. He had been a very effective
pitcher in the American League. After a couple of
years off he finally made his comeback and his
story was portrayed in a motion picture made with
Jimmy Stewart and June Allyson. They showed
how he pitched in the back yard, day after day,
hours on end, to get his rhythm back to be able to
pitch with one foot. Finally, he made it back to the
big leagues and on his first day out he pitched a
one-hitter. Now that's a burning desire. Monty
Stratton can't get in the Hall of Fame because his
record won't permit it, but certainly he will go
down in the annals as one courageous human being.

At the Beginning

Whatever you do, at the beginning of a speech, when
you use anecdotes, make them short. I've already pointed out

in the earlier chapters that one-liners are very effective when you're starting a speech. Any time you tell a long story, you demand that much more attention from your audience, and of course, if for any reason the story doesn't go well and you don't get that attention then you're starting off with a real handicap. So at the top of your speech, using anecdotes is good, but be sure that they are not too long . . . or you may lose control of your audience.

Told as True

Stories, anecdotes, incidents, and narrations, which speakers use to support their main points, are sometimes mythical, sometimes enhanced a bit by the speaker. Quite often anecdotes are those that other speakers have used and as each one uses them, they seem to become a little bit more exaggerated. Nevertheless, you should make it a point to tell your anecdotes as if they were true. There should be no doubt in the mind of the audience that what you are telling them is a true story and you need not make a reference to whether or not it is true.

You probably have heard of Myron Cohen, the night-club comedian from New York City, who was a salesman in the garment district in New York before he became a popular storyteller. After a lot of encouragement he wound up on the nightclub circuit as a comedian. In his monologue, he, every now and then, points out that this is a true story. It's all right because it adds a little to it, but some speakers would be better off not to say their stories are true or not true because it could lead the audience to believe that everything else they said is not true. You have to be very careful in doing this. You should use your anecdotes just as if they were true stories.

To Close

If anecdotes help to breathe life into a speech, to help it seem more real, to make it more believable and to support a point, then it must be true that these would work just as well to close a speech. A number of speakers place strong emphasis on their close. They usually like to use an anecdote or a story as the final support of the last point they make. More than likely it's an anecdote that bears out their belief of the whole story as given. Let's see what can be done with that type of a story. Here's one that I've used successfully a number of times.

> *A couple of years ago I was attending a convention in Charleston, South Carolina. It was a Sunday/Monday Tuesday convention and on Monday during the business day, the convention day, the authorities learned that there was a fellow there attending his last convention. He was going to retire. He had a young fellow with him and was introducing him to the customers, the prospects, the competition—everybody around the convention.*
>
> *During the day on Monday they decided to get this fellow a going-away gift, a kind of a special gift from the convention group, because he was so well known and so well liked. So someone went downtown and bought a going-away gift for him.*
>
> *That night between the banquet and the floor show, the chairman got up to start the meeting and he called back to the back of the big meeting room to bring this fellow up. As he was coming up the speaker began to tell about what an enviable record this man had established in that particular state. He had been traveling and selling for his company for 35 years. The speaker said that his man used to call on his father. His father had high respect and high regard for this man and he went on to tell why. He had ideas, he came in with a real interest in the company. As the fellow that was retiring got about ten yards from the head table, tears started streaming down his face, and the entire audience, and particularly those at the head table, could see that he was emotionally touched*

*by the tributes that were being paid him. It was a
touching scene. I looked around and a number of
people in the room had eyes that were wet too, as
mine were.*

*I began to think, boy, this is really a great
evening for this gentleman. If there's anything such
as the Salesman's Hall of Fame, I'm sure this man,
Red Garrett, is heading that way. Then I remembered that it takes more than just one man. It takes
all of the people in the company. It takes the management team who supply good leadership and
good direction for the company. It takes not only
the salesman's attention to service, but the attention of service and customer relationship from all
of the company, and if ever I've seen a happy
situation this one was it.*

Quite often when I use this story, I use it in a company
meeting, and I can say truthfully, (and I usually know by
then), "This to me, seems like the kind of situation you have
here—management who wants to lead well and salespeople
who want to perform well—and I commend you for this
happy relationship."

Then I take my seat. This anecdote, not too long, but a
good way to close, covers again the good points of leadership: the good points of dedication and desire and ties them
together; the salesman with the sales management team in
general; a good company, with good people and good products to sell, going about their various activities in an honor-
able way to make it possible for the customer to be served
properly. It usually is a good closing for me when I choose to
make that particular close. I use it for company meetings, but
it can be used otherwise.

Examples, Examples, Examples

I have tried to point out in this chapter on anecdotes that
your speech is no good whatsoever if you don't put some real

life examples into it. Examples are good because you need to talk about people by name, if possible. As you've noticed, a number of the anecdotes that I have described in this chapter use real people called by name, create attention and interest, and maintain control.

Watch for an opportunity for anything that may be happening within the industry that's newsworthy. If possible, work it into your talk. It's instantly recognizable and it shows the people, the meeting planners as well as the audience, that you are particularly interested, that it's not just a canned speech and in no way can be changed, that you're up to the minute with it.

It's also important, when possible, to use current events, because modern businesspeople who go to the meetings or conventions today are keeping up with what's happening across America, and in fact, across the world. If you can tie into these things it will not only help you relate to them, but the audience will be thinking, "Look, this person's well-read, no wonder he's programmed for our meeting. He's on top of things. He knows where he is."

Your anecdotes can be the down-home type example that supports a point. The important thing is to use examples, use anecdotes, use real-life stories. Real-life stories make it more understandable and more relative to the audience you're addressing. Wherever possible, use the names of famous people, such as Paul Harvey, Dr. Norman Vincent Peale, Dr. Joyce Brothers, Earl Nightingale, people in the government or well-known authors. You want your audience to know that this is not just a theoretical example, and that you have the ability to tie in to their way of life to make your message fit them.

Keep in mind that when you use examples and anecdotes, not only does it breathe life into your talk, but it helps you, the speaker, to take it out of the theoretical stage and put it into real life, which is what an audience is looking for. If they wanted it the other way they would just read the material that you have to read, in order to be well informed. They could just stay home. That's why reading a speech to an audience seldom does well, because the audience could well say to themselves, "I could just read it myself and wouldn't have to make this trip."

Name Dropping

Here again, if you're going to use names throughout your talk, even if it's not in a particular anecdote, if it's a simple statement and not much of a story or case history, then use the names of famous people because they are instantly recognizable.

Sports figures are always quotable. They can be used not only humorously, but in the desire for improving lifestyle, drive, and achieving excellence. These are usually exemplified in the lives and the happenings of the famous sports figures that you know about and hear about.

Today you could be talking about Jimmy Connors or Chris Evert Lloyd; they're instantly recognizable. Again in the summer months it might be well to think in terms of using quotes of other tennis or baseball players.

As you come into the fall, quote or use an anecdote about a famous football player or coach such as Bear Bryant or some of the currently famous people. Keep in mind that you have to relate it in more ways than one to your audience. You've constantly got to establish this rapport to maintain control.

As I've said before, this book is about delivery. When I talk about delivery, that does not include such things as stage fright and most preparation. However, you must be quick to recognize that your anecdotes should, to some extent, be planned, but the skillful speaker, the accomplished speaker, has a collection of anecdotes that he or she can call on instantly to help his or her audience relate. These may come without any preparation. Because of that it's important that you know the story well so that it can be given in story form and certainly never read.

Think of the best speakers you've ever heard. If you can remember how they delivered, you'll find that every accomplished speaker who becomes known as an effective speaker sprinkles his or her talks with anecdotes. He or she may use humorous anecdotes; he or she may use interesting anecdotes. Chances are he or she will use a combination of both, because it's the one thing that is instantly recognizable and believable when you begin to tell an audience about the success of another. It's more believable than anything you could ever put in the way of theory. Anecdotes are important. They may be humorous or just interesting, but they must be forceful. They must make a point.

Dramatize

It's important that when you tell a story, you tell it with feeling. You may be making some points that you feel very strongly about. It is never good to make speeches about which you don't have a strong feeling. Whatever you do, breathe life into your stories, perhaps by occasionally using a *stage whisper*. The stage whisper can be heard in the back row and you can see how it gives feeling to your words. If perchance you're talking about enthusiasm, for goodness sake act enthusiastic. If you're talking about confidence, sound confident. Let your voice and your mannerisms and your delivery in every way exemplify the passage that you are covering. If you ever noticed a speaker telling about something that you have a lot of feeling for, but for some reason or another the speaker didn't seem to care about, you know what I mean. So whatever you do, give it feeling—let it show. When you do this, you need not worry about the story being listened to and heard.

If you are to master the power of audience control, you will become good at storytelling, using case histories, using examples, and using anecdotes, both interesting and humorous!

Jeanne Robertson of Burlington, North Carolina, "the tall girl with a tall sense of humor," uses her own personal examples throughout her hilarious talks. She is one of the most popular speakers on the professional circuit today and is truly in demand for keynote, luncheon and banquet appearances. Almost all of her talks are filled with anecdotes about her life as a tall woman. She found the real humor of her height early on, and has regaled audiences across America with hilarious stories about her youth, her teenage years and the funny incidents that continue to take place daily as she travels to and from her speaking engagements.

*****

And now for a little levity . . .

8

Making Humor
Pay Off
For You

No one is born funny . . .

Humor can be learned, practiced, and applied by anyone willing to try. If you can employ humor properly, it is a highly desirable tool. It displays to the audience that you are likable and helps you sell yourself to the audience. Using humor calls for a light-hearted, buoyant, jaunty disposition. You must appear to be in high spirits.

Most of the best speakers use some humor in their talks. They may cover a very serious subject, but they will still use humor. They place it properly so that the audience can have a letup, so to speak, from the serious message. The audience must have a "breathing spell" occasionally, and humor provides this opportunity.

Humor may also be used to tie various points of your speech together as a transition method, to enable you to move from point to point smoothly.

Why Use Humor?

How does humor help a speech? Why use it? For one, to be honest, too many speeches are too dry and too dull. It still may be the type of message that needs to be given, but it's highly desirable to at least break it up occasionally with a bit of levity, just to let the audience relax a bit from a very serious message.

It is quite difficult for a speaker to go on making point after point of a very serious nature and still be able to keep his or her audience interested and alert. Humor can help cover these dull passages, these more serious parts of a speech, and still make the points that must be made. It is possible to make only so many points in any given speech, so humor can be used between these points to keep the control and attention of the audience.

Must Relate to the Audience

If it is a professional group, stories that relate to their profession are recommended. If it is a business or trade group, such as a state, regional, or national convention, it is good to relate at least partially to their main interest.

In addition to trying to relate your humor to the group's particular interest, it is always effective to make humor relate to people, to the changing times, to current lifestyle. Regardless of the particular audience, these subjects are important to them. Instant rapport can be established and humor helps in a big way to hold the interest of the audience, and therefore, help to maintain *control* of their thinking.

A Story Misses

What if your attempts at humor, at storytelling, at levity, fall flat? In short, your stories don't go over; the audience does not laugh. They just sit there. Apparently they did not think the story funny, or you did not tell that story particularly well. They have to first get the story clearly and your delivery of it must be well rehearsed and timed. One-liner humor is good to use for this reason. If you tell a rather long story and fail to have one or two humorous break points within the time used to tell the story, and at the end of the story they still have not laughed, your humor has *bombed*.

To the inexperienced speaker this is a catastrophe, but it need not be. I will not go into the method used by comedians called *savers*, because it is not intended for use by the infrequent speaker. However, it is important to note that if an attempt at humor fails, you must go on with your message, because after all, you are not billed as a humorist and should not let this unsuccessful attempt at humor throw you. The message delivery is the main purpose for your being there.

This failure to get expected laughter happens to all speakers, even seasoned professionals. The professional speaker has learned to expect this to happen occasionally. When a proven story doesn't go over and the audience just sits there with a cold look on their faces, they still understand. You must remember this, you cannot let it disturb you, and you cannot let it discourage you from further attempts at humor.

If you have one-liners or short stories later in your speech, by all means go ahead and use them. You may have just missed on that one story. After all, one humorous story, one funny line, does not make a speech; the important fact is, don't let it throw you, just keep right on.

I doubt if anyone can explain why a really good story sometimes fails to go over. It may be a story that you've used successfully in other speeches, or you may have heard other speakers use it successfully. You must not let it ruin your whole talk. This happens to everyone, so go right ahead with your speech. Whatever you do, don't apologize; and don't even mention it if a one-liner, or a humorous story fails to go over.

Keep in mind that this is part of the challenge of public speaking. It's difficult to explain and can seldom be anticipated. The real purpose of your being there is to deliver your message. The success of a speech does not and should not, depend totally on the humor that you've planned for the purpose of giving your talk the light touch.

Breakfast—Lunch—After Dinner

At a breakfast, luncheon or dinner, humor is needed even more than it may be in a keynote talk or a talk within the middle of the program. There is something about speaking while the audience is still seated following a meal that calls for more humor.

This need for humor is particularly true at a banquet. The program planners usually will tell you that this is an after-dinner spot and they would like to have a speaker who can use humor. Usually they will ask for humor with a message, so if you accept an after-dinner speaking date, whatever you do, be sure that you are prepared to give it the light touch.

As you become more experienced as a speaker, you should begin to gather additional stories to support any part of your speech. Review it frequently, especially before each speaking engagement. You will become so familiar with your collection that you can call on a story, or a one-liner or two, that you really hadn't planned to use. Your skill as a speaker will indicate that this may be a good spot for it and it just comes out for you at the proper time. It may take the place of a story that you planned to use, or it may be in addition to what you had planned.

The Proper Mix

Quite often after a speech, some of the audience will come up and thank you for being there, shake hands, and tell you they enjoyed your talk. Quite often they will mention one or two stories that you told. If they fail to mention any of the content of your message, then you quite possibly could **have failed as a speaker to deliver the message you were** asked to give. So whatever you do, don't let humor take over. Don't let it become the important part of your speech, because if you reach that point maybe you should consider becoming a humorist. There is a limit to the amount of humor an industrial speaker or a speaker addressing a profession should use. Time and experience should dictate the proper mix.

Humor File

Speakers who speak frequently and want to improve their techniques with the use of humor usually have a special file set aside with their speech material that they label, "The Humor File." In this they collect stories they've heard from others; anecdotes, one-liners, or short humorous statements that they feel at some time will fit into their programs. They will keep it up to date and this file will continually grow. Good speakers understand humor better from this collection of material and they study it and constantly think of where and how they can use it. It's important if you want to get better in using humor that you have your own Humor File.

The source that has been best for me is the service of:

QUOTE
Suite 100L
215 Piedmont Ave. NE
Atlanta, Georgia 30308

This comes out every other week. It's current. It has humorous lines and short stories gleaned from America's best known newspapers and magazines. Other good sources for current humor are:

Comedy and Comment
447 N. Mitchner Avenue
Indianapolis, IN 46219

Orben's Current Comedy
700 Orange Street
Wilmington, Delaware 19801

In my library are some 25 to 30 books on humor. I've studied these books carefully and have used many stories from them but quite often the best stories that I use come from one of these three publications, plus stories I've heard used successfully by other people, not necessarily professional speakers. These are collected and categorized and they help me to keep current in what's happening across America that can be used as humor.

Proper Application

Very few of the top rated speakers of America attempt to give a speech totally without humor and there are very few part-time speakers who use humor effectively. There is a reason.

The speaker, who is just starting to think of spicing up a speech with humor, doesn't realize how important it is to know the story well. Sometimes attempts are made to actually read a funny line, or a short, humorous story. This is absolute suicide. You simply cannot read a story to the audience and get the response you need. One exception could be a funny letter or a funny answer in a column that you could read, to point out from where it came. Humor has to be told as a story, even a one-liner, and you have to look at your audience to do it successfully.

It is doubly important that you prepare when planning to use humor. Frequently, friends will ask me how to be a better speaker and how to use humor to help them become a better speaker. I always tell them, that when they are getting ready for their speech and if they have only a short time to rehearse, to practice any humor that they plan to use. By all means let that be the thing that you rehearse. Say it out loud over and over. With humor, it's all in the timing.

Study the Comedians

Watch Bob Hope. Remember just the look that Jack Benny used to use. Watch and study George Burns. Notice how they use their remarks and how their body language and facial expressions help sell the punch line. It is a very difficult part of speaking. Humor in speaking always gets better with experience and with rehearsal and practice. Practice and rehearse your stories and one-liners before a mirror and you can improve your facial expressions, your body language, and your timing. This will pay big dividends when you face the audience.

Who Can Use Humor?

Who can use humor? Anyone who will work at it! However, it is like selling and like speaking. For some humor comes easy, for others, it does not. Whatever you do, if you plan to improve your speaking ability, learn to get better in using humor by watching others who are good at it. Possibly you'll be on a program with another speaker who is extremely good with humor or telling stories. Study his or her style, but do not try to imitate.

Another good method is to study manuscripts when they are available to you. Even better, get a recorded cassette of a good speaker's method of delivery. You can learn a great deal from studying this type of material because you will tell just from the sound of the voice, even though you cannot see the speaker, how they are making their humor pay off for them.

Sometimes it's a pause. Sometimes it's the spacing of the words. Sometimes it's the accent on certain parts of a funny line. Anyone can use humor if they practice. Recognize its value in speech making; you must understand and appreciate how humor can help you maintain audience control and speaking power.

Study the Platform Humorist

Joe Griffith of Dallas, Texas, a former actor, and still active in TV commercials, is extremely popular on the luncheon and banquet circuit. Those who know enough about speaking to judge his ability as a speaker always notice his timing. His rate of speech is carefully measured, his pauses are keyed appropriately, and his facial expressions always match his tone of voice, so that the audience is prepared and waiting for his punch line. This is timing. This is conditioning your audience to laugh.

Dr. James "Doc" Blakely, CPAE, another funny guy from the great state of Texas, the home state of many great humorists, is another humorist that every speech student, especially those interested in humor, should try to hear. "Doc" finds the humor in day-to-day living and has a great time telling his audience about it. "Doc" is known for his clean humor—as any successful speaker must be—but he is especially remembered for the fact that he enjoys it. He has a good time telling his stories. It shows. It's magic. He enjoys it and this helps the audience to enjoy it.

Make It Relate

It is important that your attempts at humor fit the subject. The humor must be related. You cannot just reach out and tell a story in between your serious points and call it humor.

A few years ago I participated in a convention in Canada where a famous hockey star was on the program. Actually, I was the banquet speaker and this sports figure was the luncheon speaker, but I sat at the head table during his luncheon talk. He was a good storyteller, but his stories were the type that go well in the locker room. He would tell a joke and then start another joke by merely saying, "And then there's the one about . . ." and he'd tell that story. Then he'd come back with "And then there's the one about this. . . ." Even the stories were not tied together, let alone being a part of his speech.

He was famous in the area and respected as a sports figure, but his speech fell flat because they realized that he was merely telling stories and hadn't really prepared for them. They did not particularly want to hear just one joke after another with no bearing on the program.

Understand the Audience

It is very important that you have a thorough understanding of the audience. This applies to any type of speech, but you must know even more if you plan to use humor. Today's humor is no doubt somewhat more spicy than humor used to be. This has been brought on by the type of humor shown on television and in current motion pictures. Almost any audience will accept more suggestive humor because of having seen it in so many television programs and in fact, all media, including daily newspapers. But, be sure you understand the audience as you plan the humor you will use.

It should be very obvious that humor, or stories told at a convention or a banquet of professional people, might not be suitable for a church banquet or a church social. Needless to say, this means that you *must have* various kinds of humor to use.

It is extremely important that you study the audience as it relates to the humor to be selected. You should also be aware of this as the humor is actually delivered, so that it can come off well. Ask questions: How many wives? How many career women? What is the age range? Get answers to these questions before the meeting. Some of these answers will come as you are waiting to go on, sometimes even after you start. You must know as much as possible about your audience.

Plan Your Humor

When I say, "plan your humor," this means that before your meeting you should give some thought to the humorous stories you expect to tell. You plan where to tell your stories, your jokes, or your one-liners. Very little humor or funny

material is ad-lib; in fact, I would say practically none is. You
want it only to seem ad-lib. A witty speaker with a keen sense
of humor will probably use some funny lines, or mix in some
humorous remarks based on what is happening in the meeting room at that particular time, or what has happened on the
program before him or her, but for the most part, humor is
planned in advance. Perhaps you could identify or mark in
the margin of the manuscript, if you are using a manuscript,
where humor is appropriate. If your talk is in outline form, a
key word that reminds you of that story could be inserted in
its proper place in the outline. Humor seldom happens just
because a speaker has a fine sense of humor.

Another reason for planning humor as you plan your
entire talk is that you can never tell exactly how your speech
will be received. In front of an audience is a lonely place if
you haven't planned properly for the occasion, and the talk
doesn't go as well as you'd like it to go. Good use of humor
can help immeasurably in saving a speech for you, if it is
planned, rehearsed, and if you keep your cool and deliver
your stories and one-liners with confidence. Effective humor
can help you keep *control*—both yours and the audience's.

Dialect

Here's a word of warning about dialect. You should
never attempt to use dialect unless it can be brought off
exactly as it should sound. The nightclub comic or the
stand-up type of performer can use dialect very effectively.
The average speaker, who is not a professional speaker and
who speaks infrequently, is not likely to be skilled in the use
of various dialects. There are few exceptions, so be very
careful.

Jokes Versus Humor

As pointed out previously, telling jokes, even good
jokes, is not the same as humor. This is often confused. It's

true that there are stories, one-liners, and good jokes that help you to make a speech sparkle. You really don't have to be funny to use humor effectively, but it helps.

There are so many places to find stories: TV, newspapers, and magazines are all good places to search. When you read or hear a story or a one-liner, you should ask yourself this question, "Is this suitable for the type of talk that I give? Is this suitable for my profession? My industry? Is this story or this bit of humor suitable for me to use either in a forthcoming speech or to put in my speech file for future use?" The more experience you gain in collecting humor, the better choices you will make.

Jokes are one thing; humor is another. Telling jokes is really the retelling of jokes that someone else has created. Humor is more likely to come from the mind of a person who has a keen sense of humor. Will Rogers was a humorist. Herb Shriner was a humorist. They saw the humor in the day to day living of America.

Dr. Charles Jarvis, CPAE, the former dentist of San Marcos, Texas, is considered by many today to be the funniest speaker in America. He is a modern-day humorist and it all began with his ability to see the humorous side of his profession, dentistry. He is hilarious and all speakers who have heard him rate him as the best. This man creates humor and therefore is not one who merely tells jokes. The National Speakers Association has awarded him their highest honor as a humorist, and he also received the coveted Mark Twain Award from the International Platform Association, given only to those who exemplify humor at its very best.

Other Speaker's Material

Many stories are told by more than one speaker. It may be the same story or same content, but one speaker can often get better results with it than others. This may be the result of where in the speech the story was used and how well-planned it was before using. It may also mean that it fit the speech better. It could be because the speaker's timing was better.

Using humor, anecdotes, or one-liners heard from other speakers is practical because all speakers have a dreadful fear of using humorous material for the first time. Experienced speakers seldom fill a speech with a great deal of new humorous material. They like for the material to have been tested, so they add new material a little each time. When a speaker borrows humor from another, they rationalize by thinking, "Well, it was probably borrowed from someone else." The truth of the matter is, it probably was.

Milton Berle has always been rated as one of America's funniest men and is known to be a notorious material stealer. He is kidded about this by his peers and he just laughs it off.

Another famous professional speaker, Cavett Robert[2], actually tells his audience as he delivers a message with humor, "I steal a great deal of my material, but rest assured, I steal only from the best. Therefore, I'm giving you the best of the stories on humor that are available today."

Don't Imitate

Probably the most dangerous thing for a speaker to do is to attempt to imitate another speaker, comic, or comedian. This could be suicide. It's highly important that you be yourself. You can, through research and practice, become a more humorous speaker by practicing the good techniques employed by the professional speakers.

Locker Room or Water Fountain Humor

It is stretching a point to call this humor. More than likely it is too suggestive or too off-color to use in a speech. You must avoid using the dirty story heard around the water cooler or in an undertone in the locker room. However, sometimes it can be cleaned up and changed to suit your

---

[2]CPAE—Chairman Emeritus of NSA

purposes. Just remember, any time you hear someone telling stories, listen—there may be a way to use it in an acceptable manner in one of your speeches.

As a Conditioner

The early chapters said that if you can get an audience to laugh together, you can get them to listen together. Humor has a tendency to hold your audience, to pull them together as a unit, rather than just so many listeners sitting out there together, but not thinking together. Humor is a good conditioner, and it paves the way for you to have all of them listening to all of your message.

Humor has a tendency to make your audience feel relaxed and this goes a long way in helping you to speak in a relaxed manner. Humor used as a conditioner is a very valuable part of your speech for it relaxes you, relaxes your audience, and helps you to get and maintain *audience control* and speaking power.

For Transition

As you deliver a speech there are a number of transition points within that speech. Quite often humor can be used as the transition point or at least pave the way for a smooth transition. Quite often a funny story or even a one-liner can be used at the end of a short passage or vignette to help you set up the next passage. It can also be used to help close out the thinking on the passage you have just covered, and help you get ready for the next. This is not to say that the various points in a speech should be set off from the others, it simply means that you flow from one into the other.

Personal Humor

It is often good to use what is called personal humor, i.e., stories, one-liners, or anecdotes, about yourself, provided this humor is not an attempt to set you up on a pedestal. Humor of a personal nature is ideal for use to gain a bit more humility. That's why it is used at the top of the speech so successfully. Using it at the top helps you to say to the audience, "I'm just a regular guy who has been asked to speak here." While you never lose your authority figure, it does have a tendency to keep the audience from feeling that you expect them to look up to you. Jack Benny was one of the greatest as far as using humor to poke fun at himself. It worked like magic for him for a long and illustrious show business career.

Satire

Satire in speaking is a delicate technique. It's good for the nightclub or stand-up comic, such as Don Rickles, who uses the put-down as his total approach to humor. Rickles is always picking on someone in the audience, and the more famous, the more forceful his lines become. He doesn't dodge anything or anyone. In fact, he brags about the fact that he insults everybody. Story after story is told about how celebrities will get into his audience hoping they'll get a little insult from Don Rickles, and therefore recognition. But this is a very dangerous technique for any speaker, so beware. Don Rickles may be one of only two or three who can bring it off.

Wit

Wit is spontaneous. Wit is unrehearsed. Wit is on-the-scene comments or thoughts that come to the speaker's mind and that may be humorous simply because he or she is a witty person. All speakers who use humor will get to be known as wits, but probably these are exaggerated compliments, because very few speakers can truthfully claim wit. There's a reason for this. The reason is that all professional speakers never trust to luck—they know that their one-liners or their attempts for laughter must be planned and carefully placed within their presentations.

Wit will certainly help any speaker to be humorous and to be liked. But there is a tendency in using wit that allows the speaker to appear to be pompous. If wit is used in speech making, then that wit must be honed carefully so that no one will be hurt by it. It is important that it be analyzed carefully to see that it is not an attempt to place the speaker at a higher level of intelligence than his or her audience. It's a very delicate area and must be carefully thought out before using.

Funny Stories

In telling funny stories, the important thing to keep in mind is that if it is a funny story with any length, it must be interspersed with an opportunity for a chuckle or laugh. You see, television today has so much comedy and so much humor of all kinds, that audiences are preconditioned; they expect to be amused rapidly and often. So, whatever you do, be sure that there is an opportunity or two in the telling of the funny story to give the audience an opportunity to laugh. It may not be the best laugh of the story, because usually this comes from the punch line, but it does help to break up a lengthy story if there are opportunities for the audience to laugh before you get to the end.

Closing Humor

Closing a speech with humor is questionable. Most speaking authorities recommend that a speaker not use humor to close. This would be particularly true for the infrequent speaker, the speaker who is not necessarily meant to be funny but is merely using humor as a technique to serve various purposes as covered in this chapter.

The totally humorous speaker, using humor at the close, is entirely different. There are good examples of how to use this, and for the nightclub comic or comedian there's an old adage, "always leave 'em laughing." This is highly desirable in a speech, if it is meant to be a humorous speech.

It's yet another thing to think of using humor at the end

of a speech when you really have used very little humor in the main body of the speech and the purpose of the speech was of a serious nature. It would take an extremely skillful speaker to use humor to close, unless, of course, that speaker is billed, scheduled and announced well in advance as a humorist.

Believe in Yourself

Your first requirement is to believe in yourself. You must believe that you have the ability, and understand the circumstances, the audience and the story well enough to breathe life into it in a humorous way.

Secondly, you must believe in the story you tell as being amusing, as being funny, as being something that would tickle the funnybone of your audience. If you don't believe in it yourself, you fail because you cannot be forceful, you cannot take charge. If you don't believe in your material, you will fail at all attempts at humor.

The experienced speaker doesn't become afraid and decide not to try humor again if he or she has a line fail. It's important that you continue to believe in yourself and your ability to use humor if any degree of success is to be maintained.

The skillful speaker, one who is trying to improve constantly, will be looking for new humor. He or she will have a good supply of humor to use in various speeches so that he or she should have no problems.

Memorize

Memorize the jokes and the humor. If you are a speaker and you want to use an outline or index cards, or if even a full manuscript and humor is to be used, place your eyes on the audience and look around the room as you deliver your humor. If you don't, it will certainly not sell. You cannot read humor. You must do what all accomplished humorists and comedians do and that is to memorize your story line. It gives it spontaneity. You have to be conversing with your audience when you are delivering humor. Look them in the eye when you deliver that laugh line, otherwise you flop miserably. Wait it out! "Hang in for your laugh," Robert Orben says.

If a tiny instance of silence follows the joke, don't let it throw you. Don't race on, fearing that you've bombed. This kills your chance for a laugh. Tell your story, tell your joke, use your one-liner, and *wait* for your laugh. This is essential. It takes guts. It's timing! It takes guts to be a speaker in the first place. If you fail at this, then you will probably fail all the way around.

Repetition

One of the main keys to being skillful at using one-liners and humorous stories is the understanding that the more you tell a story, the better it becomes. Now it's true that after a while you will get a bit tired of a story and you may want to drop it for that reason. The important thing to remember is that all of those people you've heard, who use humor effectively, are using some of their stories over and over and over. They practice and get better at telling them because if a story or a funny line is good for a laugh last month, chances are it's good for a laugh this month, if you tell it well and get your timing right. So don't be afraid to use a story again and again and again. Don't worry; your audiences will let you know when the time has run out on a story. You'll be given plenty of warning—you'll know that it's time to drop it and find something new to replace it.

Levels of Sophistication

What could be called sophistication, as it relates to the use of humor, is much more universal than ever before. The constant barrage of sophisticated comedy on television, in magazines, newspapers, and, in fact, in every walk of life, has made all audiences somewhat conditioned. No longer is it necessary to use a particular brand of humor with a small town group and then use something entirely different for the big city group. They are now very much alike. This applies particularly if you are commenting on today's lifestyle, the times in which we are living, etc.

Through the years Bob Hope has been a master at understanding what the American people are thinking. He has been able to use humor in such a way that it applies across the nation. If he can do his stand-up routines on national television when people of all walks of life are listening and laughing, then you, the speaker, need not worry too much about the level of sophistication of the various audiences that you may be called upon to address.

The educational level may be different and therefore your stories and word usage may be different, but a level of what the American public will laugh at need not be a problem to the speaker any longer.

What's Funny

This is an interesting question. What's funny is really what makes someone laugh. Today that could be about anything—anything about people, about current events, about lifestyle, about politicians—whatever is likely to amuse your audience.

Someone wrote that Sigmund Freud became extremely interested in the phenomenon of laughter. He studied it from all angles; analytically, scientifically, ultimately deciding that laughter was based on tactile stimulation. He tried to make babies laugh but no amount of talk or special bits of witticisms had any bearing, but once he tickled the bottoms of their feet, they laughed. That's how he arrived at his conclusion that what makes people laugh is what's funny.

With audiences you stimulate minds to get them to laugh. You do this with the clever use of funny stories and funny material. This is what gets people to laugh. Any research that goes deeper than this is likely to be confusing. You know that some people laugh readily at times and at other times more reluctantly. So the important thing is to understand that what is funny is what makes people laugh and that is the kind of material effective speakers use.

Surprise

Steve Allen, an accomplished laugh-getter, was asked once, "What is humor?" In one word, he answered, "Surprise." The surprise ending to a story, or even to a simple one-liner, is what gets laughs for a speaker. That is why timing is so important in the delivery of humorous material. You build toward the punch line, and give it a humorous twist that tickles and amuses your audiences.

Keep in mind that when you can get your audience to laugh together successfully, you can get them to listen together. This is the real power of humor in speaking. If they laugh together and listen together, you will maintain control. The really skillful speaker can use additional humor to regain control . . . if it appears that part of his or her audience is drifting away mentally.

Practice, Practice, Practice

In this respect, learn to watch the professional comic . . . the stand-up comic . . . the monologist. They set up one story after another. They work with a continuity to their stories or their one-liners. You can learn to do that. There are good books and services on humor that are highly valuable to you and I recommend them. Humor can be made to work. It has been done by many others. It will continue to serve speakers in a good way because it helps the speech to become more palatable to the audience, which in turn makes the audience more responsive.

Keep in mind that you must practice a story after it is

selected to get it down pat. If you take a line and make one word in it plural when it should have been singular, you kill the story. If your pause is too short, you kill the story. If your pause is too long, you could kill the story, although this is not as likely to happen as pausing for too short a time. If you garble a word, you kill the story. You have to practice to get it down pat! There isn't much that will change as far as your message content is concerned. What you have to say in the way of a message is pretty much going to come out the same way every time, but if you are going to use humor, practice, practice, practice. . . .

*****

Express yourself!

9

How to Use
the Power of
Showmanship

Make it live . . .

When you have developed a good speaking vocabulary, have learned to use colorful words with real punch and shades of meaning in order to paint word pictures for the audience, then you have mastered the arts and skills of verbal expression. A really dramatic speech presentation can be given with these skills, when coupled with the ability to give the speech with a sense of physical expression. This is the skill of using meaningful gestures as the speech is delivered.

Practically all of your body may be used in breathing life into your talk with the use of various gestures. The hands, arms, head, and facial expressions get into the act when you are delivering forcefully.

In order to fully understand the value of gesturing as you talk, just think of a speech you've seen delivered with very few, if any, gestures used by the speaker. The speaker stood robot-like and seemed mechanical. The speaker appeared to be reciting. No feelings were displayed. It is doubtful that you've ever seen good material being given in good voice without the use of gestures. To do so indicates a total lack of feeling or understanding for the subject, and that is why the gestures are missing. It is impossible to deliver a speech with real feeling without gestures.

Gestures add fluency to the delivery. When I am conducting a speech workshop, I point out over and over to those who are having trouble getting the words out, to let go with their hands, their arms, even their head, and the words come tumbling out much easier. Once I get them to let go and try to gesture a bit, the rest is easy, because they realize it does help their fluency.

Show me a speaker who is standing at attention, mouthing words like a robot, and I'll show you a person who does not understand the power of audience control. The words have no meaning, chances are they are in a monotone; most likely it is being read, and if not, then it comes off as if that person is reading.

A eulogy is something different. Even so, the speaker may still use slight gestures but would no doubt be delivering the meaningful thoughts in such a reverent manner that really forceful gestures would not be expected or appreciated.

Breathing life into your talk with well-placed gestures gives it meaning and drama. Without these two ingredients, why should anyone listen? Gesture freely as your feelings call for them.

Posture

Let's be sure of what posture means as you deliver the speech. It's important that you look in command as you stand at the podium, as you direct your attention to the audience. Stand erect, do not hunch over. Stand straight, and generally, it's best to balance your weight on both feet, but don't appear immovable.

Think of an army career person who has been trained year after year to stand erect. It appears as if they are in command of the situation and their surroundings. This is how a speaker should appear; in charge and in command with a degree of flexibility. The important point is to *be aware* of your posture, so your body language will show in your favor and not against you.

If you slump over the podium you could be saying to the audience that you don't really have a strong feeling about what you are saying. This will not get favorable attention. Remember how important your posture is as you face an audience. You want to lead them to think as you think. Look like a leader!

Gestures

You cannot force gestures. If gestures are forced, they appear jerky, choppy, and usually indicate to the audience that you are somewhat nervous and not relaxed. Gestures, as much as anything else, help you—*the speaker*—to relax. You must not force yourself to gesture because you've heard someone say that gestures are important in speech making. Gestures come with feeling, but less experienced speakers do have to learn how to let go so that their gestures can come freely.

Gestures Come with Feeling

The better prepared you are, the better feeling you have for your subject, your audience, and the occasion, and the more likely it will be that your gestures will be directed from your mind and from your heart without you ever having to be conscious of them. Realize that gestures are a means of expression; they are a means of supporting the words you are using as you deliver your speech. Gestures are not primarily for showmanship; although they are very much a part of showmanship in speaking, they are never noticed by an audience unless they are poorly done.

The Hands

If you take your hands out of your pockets, or move your hands from your side, and let them move as you talk, you will find that not only will these gestures make your speech come alive, but you can move your hands easily and without a choppy, jerky effect.

Good, smooth gestures, with feeling that comes from the mind and from the heart, and do not appear to be part of an act, actually help you become more fluent. As you get further into the talk, you will realize how gestures help you drive home the points you are trying to make. Make sure your hands are free and ready to move, and they will move without you having to think about moving them. As you cover the points of importance in your talk, gestures will help you to make your speeches become easier to deliver.

A capable speaker will let his or her hand pierce the air to demonstrate and to punctuate certain passages. This comes with feeling, even though in the early stages many speakers have probably felt the need to think about their gestures before speaking. That will become less necessary as the speaker gains experience and learns to let go easily.

Gestures Accentuate

Gestures accentuate various words, passages, and meanings. When a carefully chosen colorful word, phrase, or strong and powerful sentence is accentuated with proper gestures, there is nothing more you can do to drive the point home. Gestures that accentuate must not be overdone because it could appear that you are bearing down too hard. Powerful, colorful language with gestures that are too forceful can become tiring to an audience.

Gestures Dramatize

Good speakers, to some extent, are actors. In other words, they have learned to put to use the skills of drama as they deliver a talk, even more powerfully, because it's the speakers own words. An actor who is acting out the words of a playwright must rehearse more to get the real meaning. Whereas, a speaker using his or her own message or passages, certainly should find it easier to put drama into a talk. After recognizing the importance of gestures and allowing yourself to move freely into your speech, gestures for punctuation, accentuating, and dramatizing should come with little or no effort. You will not remember how many times you gestured or what gestures you used once you learn to be at ease and let these physical expressions help. It is a skill that comes with time. It comes automatically once you get the proper feel for this method of delivery. As you continue to speak and gain experience, you become less "up tight" as you deliver, and you will never have to think of gesturing.

Head Gestures

Recall how Franklin Delano Roosevelt used his head to gesture as he spoke. Aides, who were with him when he gave those famous fireside chats over national radio hookup, recall how he emphasized and gestured with his head as he spoke into the radio microphone. Those talks were extremely important as he told the listeners across the nation what was being done by his administration to pull the United States out of the worst depression ever known. The fact that he used head gestures, even while broadcasting over the radio, tells you that not only are gestures very good to use as far as the audience is concerned, but they are extremely helpful to the speaker, because they help the speaker to breathe life into his words.

Roosevelt's words told us that he nodded his head, shook his head, or turned his head from side to side as he talked and delivered those messages. When he was seen in motion pictures, like the newsreel news, those same head gestures that he had used on the radio broadcasts were evident as he spoke. He also used these head gestures when he spoke before a live audience. President Roosevelt was generally credited by all who heard him on the radio, or saw him on newsreel or in person, as being one of the best speakers this country ever had in the White House.

Many modern day telecasters use head gestures as they deliver the news or in other TV appearances. It adds meaning, it accentuates and, yes, it even dramatizes.

Natural Gestures

It is important that you maintain a natural feeling for gesturing and let your gestures come naturally. Any forced gesture as you deliver a speech is likely to appear jerky and without feeling.

Observe the great speakers. They never seem to be using anything but a natural flow of their hands and natural sway of their bodies, and it never appears planned.

You should not try for perfection in gestures, even though some speech teachers recommend that you practice gestures before a mirror. This may be necessary for the beginning speaker, who has all of the hang-ups that beginning speakers have. However, once you begin to practice gestures and begin to try to memorize movements or gestures, you are likely to make them come off too rehearsed. It will give the appearance of having put them into the speech for effect. This could have an adverse effect on your audience. If they then feel that your gestures are insincere, then perhaps you are, too.

As an example, a speaker that I have heard on several occasions uses gestures that appear to have been carefully planned, written into the script, and rehearsed with feeling. This has a tendency to come off as a canned performance that does not really come from the heart. He even uses the Billy Graham two-finger gesture, which has the index finger on each hand pointed slightly upward. I've heard other people criticize his use of gestures, complaining that they are grossly overdone, and wondering how long he rehearsed a particular gesture. Learn the importance of gestures in the early stages; let your hands roam free. You will find that, once you get into your subject, there will be no real problem in using the gestures you need to use to make your speech forceful and effective and to help you maintain audience control.

Facial Expressions

It is important that your facial expressions fit the message, as well as fit the gestures you use. If you were giving a eulogy, or if you were telling a sad story, you would not be smiling, grinning, or seemingly in a joyous mood. Facial expressions reflect the words you speak, the feeling you are trying to impart.

This may seem academic, but you still see speakers who stand at the podium and never change their facial expression no matter what they are saying. They keep the same expression on their face. Two things will happen, and both are bad. The audience will get sick of that expression, and it will indicate that you really have no feeling for your thoughts, that you are merely "mouthing" the words. Good speaking as I said before, is to some extent good acting. Accomplished actors rely heavily on facial expressions to drive home the meaning of the lines they are delivering, regardless of how many times they have said those lines. They are very aware of the importance of the facial expressions, along with their gestures and their body language, so that all their actions fit their lines.

Suitable Gestures

Be sure to think of the words you are speaking as you begin your gestures. You must suit the gestures to the words, to the passages that you are using as your speech unfolds. Power gestures are used to express powerful words, such as wide sweeping of the arms to indicate an expression of power.

If you are speaking rapidly in the delivery of your

speech, then your gestures should be quicker, but still not choppy and jerky.

If you are speaking about religion, then it would seem that the gestures should go upward rather than sideways or downward. The gestures should indicate that you are talking about that all-powerful God above.

Gestures lend emphasis, just as they punctuate, accentuate, and dramatize. When you use a gesture to stress a point, that gesture should be delivered in a more deliberate manner than others. Gestures sometimes are used to change pace in your talk and even as a transition point from one passage to another. If a gesture worked well the first time there is no reason why it could not do so again.

Don't Overdo

It never looks good for you to stand with both hands in your pockets for any period of time. I have seen very effective speakers stand at the podium and have just one hand in their pocket for a few moments and use the other hand for gestures. After a bit the other hand goes to work and one either rests at his side or slips into his pocket. This is just being natural; it is not terribly wrong. The important thing is to let go and don't be nervous about it.

It is so easy to overdo gestures. If you are not extremely careful you will begin to look like all hands and arms, and this in itself could become distracting. When a speaker gestures too frequently it may mean that he or she is not sufficiently prepared, or that the message is not going over too well. Be careful that you don't get into the habit of overdoing your gestures, because it may seem to the audience that you are attempting to force your ideas on them.

Body Action

It is not good style to move around behind the podium, but you should be natural and let your body help you with gestures.

When using a lavaliere microphone or a hand microphone, moving around is in good form and is expected. Many professional speakers like to deliver in this way and they make the most of their freedom to move as they emphasize and use their movements to add excitement. It is a form of body language. It is especially effective in an inspirational or motivational-type talk.

Body language has become an important study in human behavior and there have been a number of books written on it. There are also seminars on body language. The best book on body language that I've read is, *KINESICS: The Power of Silent Command* (Parker Publishing), by Merlyn Cundiff.

Merlyn Cundiff is a nationally known platform speaker, as well as a seminar leader on this subject and other management studies. She tells how important positive body language is to the speaker in letting the audience know that you are in command and, in fact, in control of yourself, which provides the power to be in control of your audience. This is good reading for all speakers who want their physical expression to fully support their message and delivery.

Keep in mind that gestures and other forms of physical expression are extremely helpful as you deliver your talk, and this added effectiveness enables you to maintain audience control. . . .

* * * * *

And now to control your audience!

10

How to Handle
Specific Program Slots

Deliver accordingly . . .

Adjustments are usually necessary when speaking in certain specific program slots. This does not necessarily mean that a great deal of different material is needed, but it does mean that the actual delivery may vary based on the particular gathering and the time of day.

Program planners should always take this into consideration and issue speaker invitations based on the actual requirements of the time slot to be filled. This is not to say that various speakers would be restricted to only one or two type meetings, but there are some who qualify for certain parts of a program better than others.

The experienced professional usually has the versatility to qualify for several occasions. Even so, this professional would want to know in advance, if possible, the exact situation to be filled. Most meeting planners will spell out these details in the initial invitation to speak, or as soon as possible thereafter. You see, at the very outset, the experienced and polished speaker is concerned about the need to use the powers of audience control even as he or she prepares for the occasion.

Breakfast

A breakfast meeting engagement differs somewhat from any other. Quite often, breakfast meetings are planned and designed to get the people, particularly in a convention-type arrangement, up early and down into the meeting area and involved in the program for the day.

A breakfast speaker usually is expected to speak 30 to 35 minutes. It may be shorter or possibly longer, but usually in that range. The breakfast meeting is expected to be something of a dynamic wake-up type, and calls for an appropriate message. Breakfast meetings usually provide a mixed audience, so you should have the usual requirements of humor in mind. However, it must be remembered that many of the people are still a bit sleepy and some not particularly anxious to attend this type of meeting.

On occasion, I've made this comment, "You may be thinking what an early time to get up to hear a speaker." I might add, "it's kind of early for the speaker to be up speaking, but since we've all had coffee and a good breakfast, let's enjoy it."

If by chance the weather is bad, you could say, "It may be raining and gloomy outside, but like Andy Griffith used to say, 'it ain't raining inside,' so let's not let it get gloomy in here. I intend to do my part and if you will do yours, this meeting will be the start of a good day."

There are some potential problems with a breakfast meeting, particularly where a convention program is concerned. Quite often, the conventioneers have been out on the town the night before and they may be just a bit hung over. Dr. Kenneth McFarland[1] uses a line in his breakfast meeting that goes very well, "Good morning ladies and gentlemen.

---

[1]CPAE—Dr. Kenneth McFarland is generally recognized as the number one public speaker in America. He is the author of the best seller book on speaking, *Eloquence in Public Speaking*, by Prentice-Hall Publishing Co.

It's good to be with you and I want you to know that I feel like one of you. Now, this early in the morning I don't know which one I feel like but whoever it is, he ought to go back to his room and go to bed."

Keynote Speech

You may be called on to give what is referred to as a keynote speech. A keynote speech means that you are expected to set the theme or central ideas for the entire convention. Normally, you are given more information about the entire meeting and about the purpose and objectives of the meeting and what they hope to accomplish. The meeting planners hope that you can tune into that and help them get their objectives stated. When it is referred to as the keynote speech, it is usually the first speech on the program as far as general assembly is concerned.

Luncheons

A luncheon program could be anything from a civic club meeting to a professional organization that meets regularly, or it could be the luncheon part of a convention program. A civic club or a professional group luncheon meeting usually calls for a presentation 25 to 30 minutes long. Convention luncheon meetings usually are made up of an audience of both men and women. In some convention-type situations they may ask for up to 40 minutes. Like a breakfast engagement, you are speaking while your audience is still at their tables.

If it is a civic club meeting or a professional group that meets weekly or monthly, you should be aware that many of them need to get back to their offices and they have set their time accordingly. Therefore, it is most important that you stick to the time allotted you and try to finish on time.

Usually a bit of humor is expected and goes over well in a luncheon meeting and, of course, helps to keep the audience interested. Meetings such as these are usually a big part of a speaker's early experience. There are inumerable engagements such as these and planners are constantly searching for speakers to fill their program needs. It provides an excellent training experience for speakers who want to expand their horizons.

Since these club and professional organizations hear so many speakers they are experienced audience members. This tends to make them good judges of a speaker's ability, especially in the speaker's early days of a speaking career. These engagements provide great opportunity to practice the power of audience control. Many seasoned speakers got their start in this way and often reflect on the experiences they have had with such groups.

After Dinner

An after-dinner speech calls for more humor than any other place on the program. It can be a very enjoyable engagement for a skillful speaker. A message with a lot of technical facts, or with a lot of figures in it, is not too well accepted as an after-dinner presentation.

It may be a weekly or monthly banquet meeting of a professional group or a civic club. Meeting planners usually try to plan a program or message with humor.

When it is an evening program of a convention the meeting planners feel that since they've had their people together in meetings of various kinds dealing with serious subjects for the entire day, then a very humorous speech is best. However, a dynamic speech on Americanism and Citizenship may also fit very well after dinner. The strong skillful speaker realizes the challenge of the banquet speech and prepares accordingly.

The evening speech may be your biggest challenge as far as getting and keeping audience control. Noise, meeting room distractions and, in fact, all of the pitfalls covered in a later chapter are possibilities, plus the added chance of coping with one or more people who enjoyed the cocktail party more than they should. (This is not to say that this is to be expected on every evening program.)

Any speaker accepting an invitation to speak after dinner must realize there might be problems, and be prepared to handle the situation if an incident arises. The important point is to keep cool, keep your poise, and practice the various methods of audience control despite these obstacles.

If you can recognize these possible distractions before your speech begins, my recommendation for coping with them is to more or less get yourself psyched up a bit more than normal and deliver your speech forcefully. In this way your forceful delivery may discourage anyone from trying to get into the act, or causing a problem. If the potential source of trouble is not recognized in advance and begins after you start, as is most often the case, you should step up the tempo and let it be known that you intend to be heard. You must also reassure yourself that the audience came to hear you and not the person trying to take over.

As a Roastmaster

The roast type meeting has become an extremely popular type of meeting in recent years. This was, no doubt, brought on by NBC's Dean Martin Roast, which is usually staged in Las Vegas. These roasts are put on by celebrities from the world of entertainment. These are fun meetings and yet they serve a purpose; that of paying tribute to a person for some of his or her well-known achievements.

A roast is also a good method for giving someone a retirement dinner. The retiree can accept and take the retirement with laughs, rather than with a dinner meeting in which everyone's comments have a depressing effect. Companies are finding this to be an excellent way to honor an executive upon retirement, as opposed to the old method of a gold watch and a few remarks.

I have participated recently in several programs such as

this, serving as a roastmaster. One of these was in Texas for a retiring executive. All of the roasters were fellow executives except their legal counsel and me. We had time for only one rehearsal and the roasters were able to give the roastee a hilarious evening, all in good fun. Several remarked that it was the best way to show their love without tears. He had the last word, and put the icing on the cake.

Another good purpose for the roast is to raise money. From time to time, you will see celebrities, or well-known people, allow themselves to become the subject of a roast for raising funds for deserving causes. These are effective and worthwhile.

The roastmaster serves as something on the order of a master of ceremonies. In this case the roastmaster has the job of keeping the program moving. In between roasters he or she can use one-liners, funny stories, ridiculous stories, not only on the roastee, but on the roasters, as well. The roastmaster pokes fun at the person being roasted but it is also advisable that he or she have a number of quips to use on the participating roasters as he or she introduces them.

This is best done by the use of one-liners. These lines should relate to these people in a realistic way so that the audience can at least consider the possibility of accuracy. These lines should also be ridiculous and funny and they are all meant to be put-downs, but should not be vicious. Anyone serving as a roastmaster or roaster should observe how it's done on the Dean Martin Roast. Keep the roast moving along, keep the audience in your control.

As a Roaster

The sole purpose of serving as a roaster is for poking fun at the person of the hour, the roastee. All stories that are used should be relative to some extent; they should be ridiculous; they should not be insulting, but have a tendency to put down the person being roasted.

It is very important for the roasters to learn their material in a short period of time. The timing has to be sharp, as with any humor, but on a program of this kind it must keep moving rapidly from person to person, then back to the roastmaster, then back to another roaster, and so on. The program and the evening's proceedings must proceed smoothly without bogging down at any one point.

Normally, the person serving as a roaster would be one of 12 or 15 other roaster. He or she should listen carefully to what is being said as other roasters perform so it does not become too repetitious.

Rehearsal is in order if it is at all possible. If a rehearsal is not in order, for example, at a convention, where people are from various parts of the country and cannot get together in advance, then some preview before the evening of the roast should take place, if only for a few minutes. This would help each one get a feel for what the other participants plan to do so that there would not be too much repetition. Nothing is more boring to an audience than to have several people refer to a certain aspect of a person's life or career and keep coming back to that, unless, of course, they can give it an unusual and different humorous twist each time. Each roaster will be expected to move to and from the podium quickly and deliver his or her lines promptly. This calls for more last-minute review and rehearsal of the material to be used than for any other speaking situation, to see that the proceedings never lag, and that the audience remains attentive and responsive.

As a Panel Moderator

This again is a situation somewhat like a master of ceremonies' performance. The panel moderator needs to be familiar with all of the members on the panel as relating to their biographical information, so that proper introduction can be made. This also will ensure that questions directed to the panel go to the right person.

The panel moderator is expected to keep the program

moving, yet be careful not to cut off anyone too soon with pertinent questions that all of the audience would like to hear the panel discuss. The panel moderator should look around the room at all times to see that those people wanting to ask questions, or ask the panelist for further information, are never passed by. Keep looking over the room and when the hands go up, acknowledge them by a nod of the head, etc. Then that person who may become restless to participate in the discussion realizes that he or she has been observed and will be called on at the proper time. It calls for skill. It is worth the effort, to the panel and to the entire audience, to help the program move along as it should and still be under control.

It is also very important that the panel moderator be familiar with all of the subjects that are to be covered. For example, if there were five panelists and one of the subjects covered by a particular panelist was not well understood by the panel moderator, he or she could very well fail to give that particular subject its proper emphasis. A good panel moderator knows how to say a little bit about the subject he or she is about to introduce, but not enough to steal any emphasis from the panelist who is about to speak on that particular subject.

It is advisable for you, as the panel moderator, to learn all that you can, not only about your panelists, but also about the subjects to be covered. If one or more of these subjects are not quite clear to you, then it is important that you get busy at once and attempt to get up-to-date information on that subject. You will be glad that you went to the trouble, because panel moderators are expected to carry the show, keep it moving, and help get a great deal of information from the panelists to the people in the audience. You smoothly direct the flow of questions and answers. It is a very pleasant experience when it goes well, but if you attempt to do this job without knowing anything about the panelists, something about their experiences and expertise, and if you do not understand the subject, it could really become embarrassing for all.

As a Panelist

It is unlikely that you would be invited to appear on a program as a panelist to discuss a subject that you are not really qualified to cover. Should this happen, then you should immediately say to the program planners, "I'm anxious and willing to participate but I believe I could do a better job for you if you had a different assignment for me." You may not actually refuse to attempt it, but it would be better than to have you give excuses for your lack of up-to-date knowledge on the subject. It will not work out well unless you cover a specific subject on which you are knowledgeable.

Quite often subjects overlap to some extent on a panel program. It is important for the panelists to get together for a few minutes with the panel moderator and briefly outline what they intend to cover. If there is an area of overlap, it is not all bad, provided it is understood and it is not total repetition of a subject previously covered.

Keep in mind that serving on a panel to cover a specific subject is somewhat like preparing for a speech. The big difference is that the panelist must realize that he or she is expected to cover the subject in a very short period of time. It takes much more preparation to get the important facts worked into proper sequence, as they relate to the subject under discussion. As the program unfolds, your panel remarks will build themselves into a small speech and with very little extra verbiage.

A word of warning—don't try to cover too much when serving as a panelist, because the temptation will be to make a full presentation when time simply does not permit. Study your material carefully and be sure that you have cut down to the bare essentials.

Does humor work on a panel situation? Yes, it does. You should be skillful in watching for an opportunity to use a one-liner or two, provided it relates. You shouldn't pull stories out of nowhere, just to be funny. The panel moderator or the panelists should never get into any lengthy story or anecdotes. It is good to add a bit of levity if it can relate to the humorous side of a question from the floor, but only a very few one-liners would be in good taste.

All who appear on a panel should have a sense of responsibility as far as maintaining audience interest and control of the audience. The individual panelist does not have to feel as responsible for audience control as the panel moderator, because the moderator has been selected for his or her skill at keeping the program moving smoothly and maintaining overall control.

The "How To" Speech

When you think of the "how to" speech, you think of instruction. Normally, this type of speech is not given to a large audience. It is frequently given to convention groups in small meetings. Some convention planners actually line up a series of "how to" speeches, and the conventioner may find it possible to attend all of them at separate times by careful planning. It may be that they will have several speakers lined up to give these instructional presentations. They can be scheduled into the convention program so that a person can select the ones most important and the ones felt most needed.

This type of speech is more of a serious nature and is something of a classroom type of program. The person giving this type of speech should be known as an expert in that field. Those attending these meetings will expect to come away with better knowledge of that particular subject, because they have listened to a person who is well versed in all details of the subject.

Another way that "how to" speeches are used and are quite popular is with sales groups. It may be a sales meeting where the salespeople are given specific instructions on their upcoming advertising and promotional campaigns, or a meeting where they are told how to present new ideas and new programs that call for specific instruction to the customer.

Some sales meetings of this kind would provide for teaching their sales force how to close, how to prospect, how to manage time, or maybe even how to establish better rapport with customers. These could all be in different workshops, and the speakers would be telling them how to do a better job in these various areas.

The "how to" speech is extremely important. It is a type of speech where teaching and demonstration play an important role in getting the message over. It would not be a lecture type of speech, but would be the type of presentation where the audience might ask questions. Most often visual presentations would be included. You, the speaker, would probably use handouts and talk from these handouts as specifics are put on a chalkboard. The "how to" speech is designed with just one thing in mind—to help those people in the audience to do a better job at what they are doing.

The key to this type of program, as far as audience control is concerned, is *participation*. Every member of that audience ought to be involved, if it is possible. You must be aware at all times of who is participating and who is not, and be ever watchful for an opportunity to get into the act those who are reluctant to comment or ask questions. This can be done easily by asking direct questions. Once the entire audience realizes that you expect all of them to comment and ask questions, you gain their attention to the proceedings and, of course, put into use the power of audience control. . . .

*****

Move 'em!

Delivering a Speech
with Emotional Impact

Deliver with feeling . . .

The Motivational Speech

Many people believe that the term *motivation* is not used properly. Dr. Ernest Dichter, often referred to as the father of motivational studies, wrote a book in the mid-fifties called *The Strategy of Desire*. In this book, he talked in terms of motivating a customer or client to move in a way satisfactory to the salesperson or the person bringing to them a proposition for action.

To motivate means to move. You cannot actually move a person or an audience, but you can cause people to move themselves to greater achievements, and therefore to a more successful lifestyle, by encouraging them to set goals, to be more committed, and to practice professionalism and the other good habits of successful living.

All too often people think that a speaker can motivate an audience. This is not true. You can deliver your message so effectively that the audience will be inspired by your thoughts and suggestions so that they, in turn, will motivate themselves. It is extremely difficult to get an entire audience to act simply because you have given a so-called motivational speech.

Most any audience is usually looking for a lift, and therefore, is an easy audience to gain attention and control of and maintain that control over.

The Inspirational Speech

The type of speech, often referred to as a motivational speech is really an *inspirational* speech. This means that the speaker, in the setting down of certain steps that can be taken for improvement or for reaching new heights in a person's career, provides encouragement by supporting these suggestions with living examples to inspire action.

Inspirational-type speeches must have living examples. Think for a moment of how a minister's Sunday sermon offers suggestions to his congregation for better living, for more moral living. Without fail the minister will give real life examples to support the points and suggestions he has just made. This is inspirational speaking.

The giant sales rallies and positive thinking rallies across America, where several speakers are used to give inspirational messages, are also good examples of the inspirational type of speaking. All are speaking in the area of positive thinking, positive living, and offer ways for the people in the audience to gain by these suggestions. These speeches are always very dramatic; they are most inspirational and they can move a mass audience to better results. As in any group, all of them may not be touched, but enough of them will be influenced by these messages, which are filled with examples and case histories of what others have done to achieve more successful living and to ensure a successful response.

As an inspirational speaker, you must employ all of the skills of audience control. You can effectively use humor, which helps to maintain interest, but more importantly, helps give the audience a rest from strong inspirational and sometimes intense passages used in this type of speech for dramatic effect.

Change of pace, along with the humor, is also very helpful. Usually the inspirational-type speech is given to large audiences; therefore, it cannot be too conversational. All of the speaking skills are needed to maintain a high level of interest.

Creating Desire

The only way that an individual or the full employment of a company or an organization can reach new heights and perform more effectively is to have a desire to do better. The late Dwight Eisenhower once said, "Good leadership is getting people to do what you want them to do because they want to do it." Desire on the part of your audience can be encouraged by the inspirational type of speech.

Good speaking is good leading. An audience can be led by an inspirational speech to reach for new horizons in their careers and to set higher goals for themselves. In order to lead the audience, you must have their undivided attention . . . and you get this by practicing the power of audience control.

Examples of Desire

There are many examples that can be used to dramatize and magnify what can be done when a person has proper desire. I like to use the example of Colonel Sanders, who at age 65, already on Social Security, with less than $500 in his bank account, founded one of the most successful food chains in the world. I often add that he changed our eating habits. The proper comment here is that you are never too old. It is just a matter of desire.

I also like to use the already cited example of W. Clement Stone, chairman and principal owner of Combined Insurance Company of America. His is the type of example that can be used as you talk about desire, to inspire your audience, to help them create their own desire.

Building Enthusiasm

The late John F. Kennedy was often referred to as an enthusiastic speaker. He probably had some of the most skillful speech writers in America available to him, but regardless of who writes the lines, the speaker has to be able to deliver the speech. The speaker must have enthusiasm to get and hold the audience's attention because enthusiasm is one of the most necessary qualifications for effective speaking.

It is not enough just to be enthusiastic about your speech, about your cause, about your message, about your role in life—you must be able to transfer this enthusiasm to your audience. That enthusiasm is contagious! But there is no way you can transfer this enthusiasm unless you can control the audience. So you must not only be enthusiastic, you must be prepared to display enthusiasm with the tone of voice, gesture, body language, and every skill you can use as you deliver your speech.

What Is Enthusiasm?

Quite often I ask an audience the question, "How would you define enthusiasm?" We could break it down and find its etymology, but enthusiasm is ethereal. It is feeling good about what you have and what you are doing. It is how you relate to others and how you communicate to others. In general, it is a good feeling about what you are about. You cannot turn enthusiasm on and off with a switch. It has to be a part of your makeup.

You must feel right about the speech you are going to deliver, and the audience, and the circumstances, because you cannot fake it. There is no way to put enthusiasm into the actual wording of a manuscript, but you can and you must display enthusiasm as you deliver. When you have the ability to do this, using the speaking skills you know, then that enthusiasm, through your sparkling delivery, will be transferred to your audience.

As you think of enthusiasm in public speaking you must use a creative approach. The objective is to make your speech come alive, not just for you, but for those people in the audience. That must be your first consideration, then you will deliver forcefully.

Regardless of how much enthusiasm you have, or how many places you have marked in your speech to emphasize with enthusiasm, it is a *feeling* of excitement that must come through as you deliver your talk.

Enthusiasm is a requirement in every type of speech. Enthusiasm is on page one of every successful selling story. Speaking to an audience is simply mass selling. You will not get them to listen, you will not get them to act, they cannot gain by your having delivered a speech, if your speech is not delivered with enthusiasm. You can build enthusiasm in your speech by displaying enthusiasm as you talk, by change of pace, change of tone, and rate of speaking. All of these skills will help you to accentuate the enthusiasm you have. However, you cannot appear enthusiastic if you do not feel it from within. The stage whisper is one good example of how you can display your enthusiasm as you speak. It shows feeling.

To Build Mass Thinking

Enthusiasm is a powerful method of speech delivery that helps you to get your audience, regardless of the size, thinking as a unit, thinking and moving along in their thoughts as you want them to. Enthusiasm unites an audience. The audience can feel if others are being moved and touched or inspired with your enthusiasm.

Uniting

After all is said and done, your primary job is to unite the audience to think as you want them to and to consider carefully taking the action you are recommending or suggesting to them.

Think about how a presidential campaign is created and delivered to the people. The job at hand is to get those people to think favorably about the candidate, so that on election day, they will vote for him. After a presidential campaign you can make a study of the inaugural speeches new presidents have given. You will find that the winner always carefully planned a means for uniting the people; uniting the people behind him and his administration with nonpartisan thinking. He realized that during the campaign many people were on different sides and that now he must carefully plan statements in the inaugural address to heal wounds and bind the total nation together.

When John F. Kennedy delivered his inaugural speech, he made this statement which has become immortal: "Ask not what your country can do for you, ask what you can do for your country." You could state that sentiment in many different ways, but the late President Kennedy had a meaning, an excitement, a believability in those lines. That is why that speech has become immortal and why he will probably be remembered by that statement more than any other statement he ever made.

To build enthusiasm in your speech your power words must be placed in proper sequence. Work it into the outline, and by all means rehearse passages where you want to pay particular attention to making it enthusiastic. It will come easily if you have an enthusiastic feeling for the subject. Be sure you feel this enthusiasm and that you use examples to support your strong feeling for it. These examples must relate to the point that you have covered or are ready to cover. If it is the least bit remote it will have a tendency to be disjointed. The audience may feel that this is not how you really feel about it and you will come off as insincere. . . .

*****

Show me . . .

12

Utilizing Visuals Professionally

Make your showmanship fit

Just recently as I crossed the street at 42nd and Park Avenue, right in front of Grand Central Station in New York City, I saw a sidewalk minister talking to any person who would slow down. He used a visual presentation as he made his comments. He was talking to the people as they went by and using a flip chart to support his statements. You had to give him credit for trying to capture their attention with his visuals as he delivered his message. He wanted that flip chart to help get audience control.

In recent years, visuals have become an important method of communication to mass groups. The choice of visuals is very important to the speaker since visuals fit various types of messages in different ways. For example, if a lot of numbers are to be used, it may be well to use the flip-chart method using large numerals and not too many on each page. This would depend on the size of the audience and the size of the meeting room.

If pictures are to be used, obviously, they must be on slides to show well and give importance to color. I have seen people try to show photography on flip charts and it simply does not come off well. Only slides with good lighting and a proper screen for display will bring the best results.

Chalkboard

The chalkboard is an effective tool for showing particular words or phrases as you emphasize them. This works exceptionally well when using case studies for a management group meeting. In fact, it is a way in which part of the answer, part of the solution, can come from comments from the audience and it helps them to visualize as the discussion continues. Key words and phrases can be erased and changed as you continue the discussion and as the audience finalizes an opinion and a solution.

Motion Pictures

Seldom will a speaker want to rely totally on motion pictures to tell the story. However, a talk on transportation may be more effective if motion pictures are used; also a talk on moving machinery may be better told in this manner. The film could be stopped at an important point but generally once a film is turned on it is best to show the entire film before stopping it.

Visuals with Message

It is not enough to have beautiful attractive visuals. You must put with your visuals a good message, delivered well.

Normally, when a visual presentation is made a part of the program, humor is not too appropriate. An audience seems to settle down to a learning process when visuals are used and they do not seem to be quite as receptive to humor. However, if a humorous incident occurs, or a humorous comment is made by someone, capitalize on it; you should not display a feeling that you are uptight or too mechanical to appreciate a little levity. This aids immeasurably in maintaining audience control.

Be in Command

You must remain in command at all times when using visuals. It is so easy to let the visuals take over the meeting by having the room too dark or by having too many visuals or by not supporting and explaining the visuals properly. You should be well versed in the important facts shown on the visuals, so that support can be made by added comments as the program unfolds.

Using visuals calls for, and in fact demands, more rehearsal and more prepration than any other type of speech delivery. If it is not rehearsed and not placed in proper sequence, it is quite possible that you will not be able to hold the attention of the audience. With good planning and pretesting of the normal aids and with total concentration as the program proceeds, a satisfying combination will be brought together for an instructional message.

Care of Visuals

Experienced speakers who use visuals guard them carefully. These visual aids are checked at the beginning and again after every meeting. They must be checked to see that they are in good working order and that they project well. Audiences dislike attempting to read messages that have somehow lost their sharpness. Visuals should be kept in top-notch condition so they can be seen from all over the room.

It is important that the proper size visuals be used for the particular audience. For example, I did a meeting at the Deauville Hotel on Miami Beach for an audience of some 300 and the meeting room was rather long. The meeting planners requested that I use a visual presentation that I had available for the material to be covered, even though I could have done without the visuals.

It was a sales and sales management type of audience. First of all, this size audience is too large to try to use the seminar-workshop style, but they wanted me to try it anyway. About halfway through I could see that the visuals were not working well in that size meeting room, so I left the visuals and worked the audience with a hand mike. This helped me to regain control of the audience by not having them straining to see visuals that were difficult to see. This is an example of the wrong type of visuals as well as an audience too large for feedback. This is also an example of trying too hard to please the meeting planners, and forgetting that once you're on, the audience is the most important factor.

Keep in Tune

Whatever you do, prepare and rehearse carefully. Be sure that your words are in line, in tune, and in "sync" with your message. Nothing is more distracting to the audience than to be looking at a picture or visual of some kind while the speaker is still talking about the last scene or the next scene. Extreme care should be taken so that you stay in step with the visuals as they are shown. With a spirited, sparkling delivery, when you are comfortable with your visuals, when you don't let visuals try to do it all and you don't try to do it all, then the blend of your words and your visuals can be extremely effective. This is a superior method of communication that will help your audience remember what they saw and what you said in your presentation.

John Wolfe, CPAE, author of *Sell Like an Ace . . . Live Like a King*, Prentice-Hall, is one of America's foremost speakers on sales effectiveness. He addresses audiences of every size on sales techniques. His visuals work well in mass sales rallies as well as in smaller sales workshops. All four aces (visuals on easels) are displayed on stage or at the front

of the meeting room as he speaks. The choice of visuals are
perfect for his message; they are colored according to each
card suit, and forcefully support his message as he moves
from point to point in his memorable presentation. . . .

*****

Questions?

13

How to Handle
Question and Answer
Sessions

Your expertise is showing . . .

Some speakers actually have questions planted in the audience, to encourage responses at the end of a program when question and answer sessions are provided in the time slot. This method is not as widely used as it once was, for most speakers are well prepared to review pertinent points in the presentation, in order to stimulate questions and discussion. And most audiences realize that when a question and answer session has been provided it is for their benefit, so that if they feel the need for more information and discussion, they are not hesitant to get it. Too often, one person will try to make a speech when asking a question. There is not much you can do about this except be patient and then summarize the question for the rest of the audience before the discussion begins.

It is usually good form, in a question and answer session, to repeat each question as it is asked so that if someone in the audience did not hear the question clearly, they will not be at a loss when you begin an answer or comment.

Question and answer sessions are valuable in certain types of programs, such as the "how to" speech and the informational-type speech. It gives you an opportunity to let the audience know that every effort is being made to see that their time spent in the meeting is worthwhile.

Be Prepared

In delivering a message of this type, you should be extremely careful to review the most important parts of your talk in advance, so that additional details may be given. You can gain credibility for yourself and your cause by having this necessary information at hand. Data or extra written material can spell out the minute details better and make them much more understandable to the audience. A speech of this type implies that you are to be introduced as an expert on the subject, so be aware of the demands that could follow in a question and answer session and be prepared to speak forcefully.

Never Ignore a Question

Occasionally someone in the audience may ask a questin that is embarrassing or that you had rather not been asked. Do not ignore it. If you need time to think, just say, "We'll get back to that question in a few moments," and be sure that you do. Then proceed with other questions and give yourself time to be better prepared to answer that tough question. If you ignore the question, you lose all credibility and control.

There are some questions that probably could be asked at certain types of meetings, such as a company meeting, that are dangerous for you to attempt to answer. Even so, you cannot ignore the question. It is best to answer immediately if you can. It could be a question about pay scales or working conditions. You, as an outsider, are not in a position to elaborate, so avoid this if possible. If you cannot answer, say so. If it is something you should not get into, say, "I believe you had better discuss that question with your management."

Get Audience Help

The skilled seminar speaker is well versed on his or her subject, but wants complete involvement of the audience, so he or she will frequently call on a member of the audience to comment on a question. It can be done like this, "I have an opinion on this, but let's see what Mr. Brown or Mrs. Smith, etc., thinks; let's see what he or she has to say." This technique may be used several times in a meeting. In this way you get the audience to help with the discussion and it has a number of benefits.

First of all, it is a member of the audience contributing to a question and this is automatic credibility. This is particularly good in a sales meeting. Someone may raise a question on how to handle a certain type of customer or prospect. They probably realize you have an answer or an opinion, but when you say, "Let's see what another person thinks," it shows that you are comfortable with yourself, and that you are willing for others to take part in the question and answer session. After all, you have already made the main speech and since this is a question and answer session, it means that someone wants more information on a part of the subject. It is a very skillful technique to let the audience help. You do this simply by calling on someone, specifically, if you know them by name, and particularly if they are a veteran, or they are known by the rest of the audience to be quite knowledgeable on the subject. It is a sign of strength, not weakness, and it will be a real help in keeping your audience totally involved and under control. . . .

*****

But you never know!

14

Maintaining Audience Control When the Unexpected Happens

Keep cool! Keep control . . .

Public speaking is somewhat like show business; once the speaker is introduced, he or she is expected to carry on and fill the assignment given, even if there are interruptions and distractions. The old cliche, "the show must go on," applies to speaking just as it does to show business. "Making a speech is like flying a plane, you have to finish and you just can't quit right in the middle," is a one-liner that sums up the situation.

Many things can happen unexpectedly before you start a speech, or during the time that you are speaking. The skilled, experienced speaker, who is thoroughly prepared and mentally ready for the occasion, will not let these distractions upset the presentation. The important thing is to keep cool, don't panic, and stay in control of the situation. The *power of audience control* is probably needed more here than at any other time, because it is possible to lose the audience control that has already been gained by letting disturbances and distractions get you off the track.

When Time Is Cut Short

Occasionally, all too often in fact, you may be scheduled to cover a certain amount of time on a program and, of course, you plan accordingly. However, just before it is time to speak the program planners may say that they are running considerably behind schedule and would appreciate it very much if you would cut your speech time.

Obviously you want to cooperate and should make every effort to help. But this can be very disturbing. If preparation has not been carefully made, continuity is not easy to maintain. And remember, there is no need to mention the situation in any way to the audience, since they will not realize that cuts have been made.

You, the speaker, will have to cut the presentation as needed, probably as you deliver your talk. When the program planners want your part of the program cut, it is usually on short notice. Often this would be just before your time to speak.

At a convention at the Greenbrier Hotel in White Sulphur Springs, West Virginia, a similar request was made of me. The speaker before me had continued 20 to 25 minutes longer than the allotted time. The audience was not aware of this, which is usually the case, and just as the speaker ahead of me was ending his talk, the program chairman asked me to cut my time a little to help make up lost time.

My talk on that day was prepared in such a way that I could leave out several points and still not disturb the continuity of the text. Since this happened just before my time to speak, I had to cut as I delivered. The important thing is to not let it disturb you too much. Be prepared to have this happen occasionally. It's a good idea to consider this as you prepare a talk. Be sure that the continuity of your message would not be destroyed if minor points were left out as you deliver.

When Asked to Speak Longer

The program people may come to you and say a scheduled speaker could not make it or something scheduled could not be presented and because of this they would like you to hold the audience until break time. Again, you may be asked to do this on short notice, so you should consider this also as you get ready for a speaking engagement. This has also happened to me when one of the other speakers failed to get into town because of bad weather. I was given this request in a whisper from the chairman of the day just before he got up to introduce me. This calls for some quick thinking. It turned out all right because in that particular speech I had a great deal of backup material for every point that was to be made. I just added to the speech, making many more detailed points than I normally would have made, using reserve material that I hadn't planned on using that day. This type of program change happens to all speakers now and then, so be prepared.

Many times you are placed in a position where you could lose your cool, and ultimately lose control of the audience. The key factor here is to have extra material ready for use and be prepared to elaborate a little more than you had originally planned.

Overlap

When several speakers appear on convention programs there is sometimes an overlap of content because it's very difficult to find out exactly what preceding speakers plan to cover. Sometimes they will get into a subject that may be the main part of your speech, such as the subject of attitude or enthusiasm, perseverance or planning, or any of the basic characteristics for success in any field. When they cover two or three of your main points you are in trouble, particularly if you follow immediately after that speaker.

This possibility makes it very important for you to have reserve material for any subject on which you speak. If that previous speaker, for example, talked about your topic of enthusiasm, in order for you to get the main parts of your talk over to the audience, you could just use the word "excitement." This means pretty much the same thing but by the same token doesn't sound as if you are echoing the previous speaker. It is not in good taste to follow a speaker in a situation such as this and tell the audience that he or she gave your speech. That would be a slap at the speaker you follow, as well as the program planner. When this happens, you must have reserve material and be prepared to cover other aspects of your subject or make some additional points. The ideal way to recover would be to have a great deal of material on other subjects, but not many speakers, even the professional, can adjust that rapidly.

It would be all right, however, to say, "As Mr. (Speaker) ahead of me has said about enthusiasm, and I couldn't agree with him more. . . ." Then go on to make some additional points, using some examples and anecdotes that point out why you feel the same way.

Late Arrivals

In too many meetings there are late arrivals for one reason or another. Sometimes these people will come walking in, some even right down the middle aisle, maybe right down to the front row. This can be very disturbing to the speaker. It's not fair, but when movement such as this takes place, when someone is moving around, it is natural for the rest of the audience to pay attention to that person or persons. They look to see who the late arrivals are, where they are going to sit, and usually will follow them with their eyes and minds until they are completely settled. The important thing is to keep calm and to keep moving along with your talk so you will not lose control.

If a great deal of this happens, or if a number of people begin to come in while you are speaking and it becomes extremely noticeable and you begin to lose the attention of your audience, then you might smile and say something to the effect that, "I'm glad you made it. Come on down front, here are some seats." This will give you a break from the distraction and will indicate to the audience that you are in command, and in control of the situation, and all is well.

When People Walk Out

Yes, it's true that sometimes people leave a meeting room because they don't like what they are hearing, but you must also remember that often people have other plans; they are on a close schedule and they must leave.

The first thing that comes to a speaker's mind, when people begin to leave the meeting room, is that he or she is failing in delivering his or her message. This is not always the case. It could be a plane the people have to catch, or they have to check out of their hotel, or some other legitimate reason. There is a responsibility on the audience here. Those who feel they may have to leave (and they should know this in advance) ought not be seated down front. They should take a seat in the rear or at the side, so they can get out without having to disturb the meeting proceedings. But you can't really change this and it's just one of the many possible distractions you have to consider as you continue to make speeches.

Regardless, you must keep command and control of the audience if you are to succeed. If it isn't happening with a number of people, just let is pass; the audience will soon forget about it. It's not a good idea to carry on a conversation or to address these people in any way, letting your feelings show in such a way that might turn the audience against you. You then have an even bigger problem.

A speaker preceding me on a program one night in New York City began to recognize distractions in a small part of his audience. Actually, it was whispering and he realized he had lost the attention of these three or four people. He began to scold them from the podium and while he did not get into a shouting match it almost came to that. Instead of using other tested techniques, he proceeded to scold and belittle them. The end result was that he turned the rest of the audience against him and he might just as well have sat down right then. He lost control.

PA Failure

From time to time you will have trouble with the PA system, either getting it to work properly at the start or problems after you start. This is another reason why it is so important to check out the facilities carefully as discussed in Chapter 2.

Anytime you have trouble with the sound system, either before or after you begin, use a one-liner that can help you remain in control. You could look squarely at your audience and say as if bewildered, "There must be a loose screw in the speaker." I have used this line on numerous occasions when the microphone was not functioning properly, and it has never failed to get laughter. It is a saver that works wonders to get you past the trouble spot and keep control of the audience.

A few years ago, while doing a banquet at the famous Grossinger Hotel in the Catskills of upstate New York, the PA system failed to perform. As a matter of fact, it came on and went off several times during my talk. The audience became restless because they could hear some of my remarks and some they couldn't hear. There was no way this could have been avoided as near as I could tell. It was just one of those things that can happen when you are delivering a speech.

In this case one of the hotel employees actually worked

on the microphone right in front of me as I waited for the repairs. Finally, he got it working again and we had a laugh about it as I said something like, "It's great to have professionals around when you're in trouble." The audience seemed to be pleased with the remark. It was a frightening experience as a speaker because I was beginning to lose control of the audience!

Talking in the Audience

When people in the audience start whispering or talking, the speaker wonders if they are carrying on a conversation because of his or her lack of ability to get audience control. It may come to the speaker's mind that he or she is not delivering, that they don't like what he or she is saying and therefore there is no interest. Of course this could be the case, but not necessarily. Occasionally, it is just an unruly group of people in the audience, or persons seated close to each other, who start talking in whispers or in undertones that are heard across the meeting room.

One way to alleviate this situation is to lower your voice so they can be heard by even more people. The chances are extremely good that this will get you out of this predicament. In other words, their voices would carry even louder when you lower yours and others will begin to look in their direction and embarrass them. You could talk louder if that doesn't work, and try to drown out their voices, but this is a dangerous technique and could seem to result in a shouting match.

Another technique to regain control of the audience is to pause for a long time. You may need to take several long pauses. If the talkers still persist, you could stop completely. By this time surely someone in authority will come to your aid to avoid a complete disaster. But you must remember, "the show must go on," so in some way continue your speech.

You could attempt to handle a situation such as this in

the manner of a nightclub comic. Some comics actually welcome a little distraction. They respond forcefully. A seasoned comic would not think of going on stage without some quips, one-liners, etc., for those hecklers, or those who are not paying attention to the act. But the speaking environment is considerably more dignified, so be careful and keep your poise.

Outside Disturbance

Once in a while there may be a disturbance outside in the hallway, or in a room next door, or somewhere nearby. The noise may be so loud that it drowns out what you are saying or gets too much attention from your audience. Quite often someone in the back of the room or on the side will step outside and let the noisemakers know that a meeting is in progress, and ask them to make less noise. This can destroy a meeting and you must be alert and prepared to correct it. Speaking louder or softer will not change this. It could reach a point where you might just pause momentarily and ask if someone in the back row would please step outside and ask for quiet, so the audience can hear. A good meeting planner will immediately step to your rescue.

The important thing is to keep cool and poised so that you do not lose the respect and attention of your audience. They will understand your problem even though they become distracted by the nearby noises. A speech is to be heard, not lip-read, so do what you have to do to get the situation in hand so you can keep your audience control.

Some meeting rooms are separated by dividers. This provides the hotel or building an opportunity to section off various size meeting rooms so that several meetings can be held at the same time. There could be a dance or party scheduled in the next room that is barely partitioned off. The sound of an orchestra or the noise of the people having fun could carry into your meeting room. Most often it seems this does not happen until you are already speaking and for some reason it always seems that those who should correct it are slow in getting around to closing doors, or trying to do something about the distraction. And it cannot always be corrected.

The other meeting group might respond that they have their room rented and they are going to carry on with their party. This proximity to a party is something the program planners should try to avoid.

All you can do is adjust. Talk louder and take over. When the music first starts, say a short comment like, "Gee, that's pretty music," or "Does anybody want to dance?" or something along those lines to show that you are in command; that you are not letting it destroy you; that you are going to go on with your speech. You could actually be drowned out and you may reach the point where you have to say to the person in charge, "I'll be glad to continue but would you go next door and see if you can get them to lower the volume a little for just the next few minutes. I'll hurry with this and we'll all come out all right."

Drunks

Recently, I was speaking at a banquet at a country club and, unfortunately for me, this organization had an hour-and-a-half cocktail party. From there to dinner, I was the only person on the program. When I was about five or ten minutes into my speech a fellow seated out in the middle of this banquet room began to talk to me. I mentioned a city and he said out loud for all to hear, "Oh, I've been there." I would mention something else and he'd comment. He was commenting in a voice as loud as mine and there was no way that the audience could fail to hear what he was saying. In fact, while they were somewhat embarrassed, they were paying a great deal of attention and wondering what this guy would say next.

I'm sure they were also wondering at the same time what I would do, how I would handle the situation, if I could get out of it. Frankly, it was becoming increasingly more difficult for me but finally another member of the audience moved over and took this fellow by the arm and led him out. This is an extreme situation but it can happen, particularly in a banquet situation with such a long cocktail party.

You must remember that the vast majority of any audience is on your side. The important thing is to conduct yourself with such professionalism that you are able to keep this majority on your side. Your speech is important or you should not be on the program and somehow, regardless of the type speech you are delivering, "the show must go on." There is no other way to think.

Too Much Feedback from One Person

Occasionally in a workshop type program, where you are asking for and getting feedback from the group, one person will seem to want to be the only one speaking up. Everyone knows what causes this—the desire for attention. Sometimes a person has that desire to impress the rest of the audience by having all the answers, by being more alert. But after a while the rest of the audience begins to resent this dialogue between one person in the audience and you, the seminar leader. If you feel that the feedback is going to continue being dominated by one or maybe two people, get away from them by saying something like, "That's great and you've really got some good ideas. I appreciate your involvement, but let's see what someone thinks over on this side of the room." It is not a good situation when a strict few try to furnish all the feedback or ask all the questions. Some of the others may be a little bit slow in raising their hands or commenting and need your skill at getting them involved.

You are there to communicate with the entire group, so you—the leader, the speaker, the seminar moderator—must see that this does not continue to happen. Simply praise them a little and say, "let's see what others think." While it's not like a heckler's situation, it can at times be almost as troublesome. You cannot put to use the power of audience control if you allow one or two participants to furnish all of the feedback and dialogue.

Message Interruptions

Sometimes during a meeting someone in the room will get a phone call or a telegram or message of some kind delivered to them. Too often the messenger will not have the courtesy to deliver that message unnoticed. They may even go down the aisle asking people where is Mr. So-and-So. If the message carrier continues to search it might be well for the speaker to say, "Do you have a message for someone in this room? Let me help you find him." Then the message carrier can come to you with the note so you can ask, "Is Mr. So-and-So here? Ah, there he is right over there." You have avoided a continued disturbance. You have escaped from a situation that could take the attention away from you and cause you to lose control of your audience. Don't fight distraction; join in, so that you can handle the problem quickly and maintain control.

Real Hostility

As you continue to speak more and more, you may be in a meeting where there are some planned interruptions coming from a hostile group. Once, while speaking at a company banquet in Philadelphia, part of the group in that meeting was determined to destroy the meeting. In the middle of the audience two fellows began to talk to each other out loud. It had nothing to do with the speech or the occasion. I learned later that they were trying to destroy the meeting with a definite purpose in mind. They were resentful of some of the activities of the company and this was their method of showing their feelings by embarrassing management and embarrassing the guest speaker.

I talked low so their voices carried that much louder. I

talked loud, slow, fast, looked right at them, but nothing would change their plan. It was total hostility, though not directed against me personally. I tried to tell more humorous stories and even that failed to get results. Finally, I was forced to cut the meeting a bit short. It was a full speech but it was some few minutes shorter than I had prepared to deliver, simply because this hostile group could not be silenced.

As always, there were many good people in the audience who resented this disrespect for top management and the guest speaker. The majority of this company audience was embarrassed by the conduct of a few. This was an extreme case and one in which the determination of the troublemakers could not be deterred by the various skills of maintaining audience control.

On another occasion in Arizona I was doing a company banquet meeting and there was a person in the meeting room who had been fired that very day from this particular company. Why he was at this banquet, I'll never know, but the fact was that he was there and shortly after I began my speech he began to move around the banquet room, table hopping, and talking to people. It went on too long to suit me but finally one of the supervisory people moved over, took him by the arm and led him out. In the meantime, it was all I could do to keep control.

Those kind of things are very distracting and people will pay attention to them, not because it's more interesting than what you are saying, but because they are surprised and somewhat interested to see just how far a person will go. You could ask such a person if he or she is looking for an empty seat or for some special person, but in a situation such as this, within a company group, it becomes a little more delicate and therefore more difficult to correct.

When Someone Gives Punch Line Aloud

When using anecdotes that have been used, or humorous stories that have been around for a while, you may find someone who will want to give the punch line. Once in Shreveport this happened to me. I told a story that was quite appropriate to support a point I had just made. I knew that this humorous story had been around for a while, but it was appropriate. I prefaced the story by saying, "You probably recall the story about . . ." and I began the story. When I got right to the punch line and paused, a fellow who had been very active at the free bar, gave the punch line and gave it in a loud voice. The audience was amused and probably embarrassed for me. It shook me up a little and had a decided effect on the rest of my speech. This caught me off guard. I failed to keep my poise and in the end I paid for the error.

Waiter Distraction

Sometimes during a breakfast, luncheon, or banquet meeting, the waiters and busboys begin to clean up the tables after the meeting gets started and it is very disturbing. Cleaning up should be done before the meeting starts but it does not always work that way. You might even be asked to start speaking before the dessert is served. This would be most unusual and you should refuse, if possible.

The program planners may decide that their schedule is getting too far behind and decide to put the speaker on to struggle through. This is unfair and means that you may have a difficult time getting control of your audience. You may be caught in a situation that happens unexpectedly in which this type of distraction begins after you've started your speech. You would be caught trying to cope with the attention given to the waiters and the noise they are making. It would be difficult to stop and say, "Let's wait until they get through," particularly after the speech is started. An alert program planner will not let a situation such as this develop, but occasionally this type of disturbance can take place and is potentially disastrous to your meeting.

You must always keep in mind that you, the speaker, are on the scene to deliver a message. Very few people realize

how an entire speaking performance may be ruined by what
appears to be only a minor distraction. This means of course
that you must be alert to all possibilities. You must be prepared to do what is necessary to maintain control of yourself
and your audience. When you display real professionalism,
real poise in the face of problems that distract from your
performance, the audience will be on your side. This is a big
plus in maintaining control.

Anything Can Happen

This may seem far out but it can happen. Some part of
the raised dais, staging, or the actual speaking platform area
can collapse, slip, or fall apart. I've seen it happen to others
and it has happened to me.

One night in Little Rock, I had gotten a few minutes into
my banquet talk when, for some reason or another, the top
dais (and there were three tiers that particular night) started
to collapse. This meeting was held in a gymnasium in order
to seat an overflow audience, so the head table staging was
temporary. I actually had to deliver my speech spraddle-
legged across two boards, with my feet spread two or three
feet apart, straddling an empty place where a board had
slipped through. When it fell the audience heard it and they
either knew or suspected what had happened. I kept right on
talking and no doubt their attention was lost for a few seconds, but my speech continued. Although the audience may
have realized there was a problem, I do believe they appreciated the fact that I was aware that the "show must go on." Can
you do anything about this in advance? No. You will not see
even a trained speaker examining the staging and the arrangements made by people who are supposed to know what
they are doing. If you saw something in advance that could
potentially be a problem, then you might bring it to their
attention. Unexpected happenings can really have a bad
effect and cause you to lose out through no fault of your own
if you're not careful and prepared to keep control.

Minor Happenings

If a minor disturbance develops, such as a dropped dish or low murmuring, then it is best to ignore it. If the disturbance continues you could make a humorous remark about it and wait to see what develops.

A story is told about a well-known speaker, who was speaking from a theatre stage when a rope in the form of a hangman's noose came loose from the rafters and swung down over his head. The audience began to giggle and titter. When the chuckles began the speaker did not know what was amusing his audience. After a few moments he could see that he was losing the audience completely and noticed that they appeared to be looking above his head. He glanced up and saw the rope. Being an accomplished speaker, he kept his cool and merely said, "I knew that my speech was not going so well, but I did not realize it was that bad." The audience broke up with laughter and applause. They felt that this man was in control, was worth hearing, and they gave him their undivided attention for the remainder of the speech.

When unfair interference is coming from the audience, you should first ignore it, if possible. Quite often this distraction or disturbance will cease. If it does continue, a look right at them and, if necessary, a comment to put the heckler or person causing the disturbance on the spot, will stop them. Make them realize that they are likely to have the rest of the audience turn on them. You have seen people in audiences whisper or turn to a loud group and hush them so the rest can hear.

The heckler, a person making this kind of disturbance, must know that he or she is in the minority. The only way the heckler can win is to destroy you, the speaker, quickly, and make you lose face.

The Audience Wants You to Win

Once again, let me remind you that when you are introduced properly, the audience, regardless of the situation, wants you to do well. This does not mean that their attention cannot be taken away from you. It does mean that if you can keep cool and keep calm under trying circumstances, particularly the unexpected, such as the many unexpected situations discussed in this chapter, you are likely to succeed. You may lose audience attention momentarily, but as a skillful speaker you will get it back and get it back quickly. A successful speaker understands *the power of audience control* and realizes the importance of keeping control so the show can go on.

Thinking on Your Feet

The more I speak, the more I realize the truth of the statement Dale Carnegie made in his early teaching of public speaking in the famous Dale Carnegie courses, that "the skillful and successful speaker is that person who can think on his feet." This applies whether you are using a manuscript, notes, extemporaneous, or impromptu. The speaker simply has to be able to "think on his feet."

You have to be able to do this even without the unexpected. But when these unexpected disturbances and distractions come along, it calls for even more skill at thinking on your feet. So, it is important that you keep cool and keep calm because there is no way that you can maintain audience attention if you panic and fail to think on your feet as you continue.

The better you are prepared, the more you know on your subject, coupled with getting yourself mentally and physically prepared to deliver, the better you will be prepared to think on your feet as you speak. This is the hallmark of the skillful speaker.

Watch a professional speaker when there are distractions. He or she seems to know exactly what to do to handle the problem. Seldom will disturbances do very much damage to the professional speaker. The material is so organized, and the pro is so practiced in delivering, that rapt attention of the audience is maintained.

Somehow the professional speaker knows how to get out of trouble and continue to deliver his or her message. The seasoned speaker is committed as a professional and realizes that the show goes on regardless of what takes place.

The people in the room expect to hear a speech. The program planners have planned for you to deliver on the subject for a certain amount of time; it's in the hands of you to make this happen. This you will do because you have mastered the art of effective delivery under all conditions; you can think on your feet, change direction, and make the speech successful, regardless of the circumstances . . .

*****

Now for the ovation . . .

15

Discovering How
to Close Your Speech
with Impact

This, they will remember . .

The close of your speech is terribly important. You can have such a memorable close that you will be remembered for some time by your audience. Closing also provides a means of summarizing what you have said.

A word of warning: when using a *summary-type close,* be careful that you don't sound too "preachy." Summarize your main points briefly, and then end your talk with a call for action, awareness, or specific instructions.

It is best to give the summarizing statements just before you say your "thank you's" (if you use that method). Let your last few words or sentences be emotional or forceful, depending on the message you have given. An anecdote or story of some kind is usually good as your final word, provided your audience knows the speech has ended.

Close only once. All too often you hear speakers who reach several climaxes in their speech, leaving the audience to wonder when it is coming to an end and when the speech is over. Good material placed toward the end of a talk is highly important. Along with your voice, body language, and gestures, the speech can end dramatically and get the desired results.

It is not necessary for you to say, "—and I close with this." Merely lead into your closing remarks in such a way that your tone of voice and rate of speech indicate that these are your closing remarks; the audience will respond attentively. This transition point can be magnified beautifully by a rather long pause. When you finish a passage just before your closing remarks, let your eyes wander over the audience, pausing as you do. After this pause go into your close, and when you finish, say thank you or just sit down.

Call for Action

An *action-type close* is the one in which you ask the audience to do something specifically. In a political campaign, you would ask them to remember you when they go to the polls. If it is a referendum-type voting situation, you would specifically review what you have said and you would ask them to vote "yes" or "no" in the proper columns on their ballots. If you are a sales manager talking to your organization, asking that they break all records during the coming year, you would specifically review steps to take to improve their sales effectiveness. This is your call for action. If it is a speech on Americanism, you would close using remarks asking that the audience begin at once to be better citizens, to exercise their right to vote, to support the person who best exemplifies their beliefs. It is a call for action, and you outline what you want the audience to do. The action close is effective and is used often by successful speakers

The purpose of a speech is to get the audience to do something specific. Often a humorist will ask the audience to look on the light side of life and to let a good sense of humor help them to enjoy life.

Appeal to the Emotions

Effective speakers use an *emotion close* to get the audience to feel as they want them to feel. For example, you may be talking to a large audience about positive living, or realizing how much they can accomplish if they set goals and make up their minds to do bigger and better things. You would have to give emotional examples, citing case histories of people who have set goals and reached them. Examples may be used effectively and the audience will remember them if you have carefully built excitement into your speech and delivered it in an inspirational way. The emotional close goes with that type of speech.

Humorous Close

The *humorous close* is used less than any other type of close, except for the straight-out humorist. The old adage in vaudeville was "always leave 'em laughing." This is true with a humorous speech but it is not necessarily true with the other types of speeches we have discussed in this book. Closing with humor is a very effective way to end a humorous talk, such as an after-dinner talk, or a talk where you have used a great deal of humor. "Mick" DeLaney, of Seattle, one of America's most popular humorists, uses this close effectively to give it the light touch at the end of his speech.

> I'd like to bring the curtain down with a story about the little boy who kept teasing his parents for a baby sister. Finally his dad said, "Well, son, if you want a baby sister so badly, why don't you pray for one?"
>
> So when the youngster went to bed that night, he prayed for a baby sister. He came down the next morning and said, "Dad, where's my baby sister?"
>
> Dad said, "It's not quite that easy. Perhaps you'd better pray a little harder."

> *That second night, the boy really went all out*
> *. . . he prayed real hard . . . he came down the*
> *next morning . . . and still no baby sister.*
>
> *He decided the idea wouldn't work, so he for-*
> *got about it.*
>
> *A few months later, his dad came to his room*
> *in the middle of the night, got him dressed, drove*
> *him to the hospital, and took him to the maternity*
> *ward. There in the bed lay his mother, and in her*
> *arms was a little baby dressed in a pink blanket. He*
> *took him around to the other side of the bed, and in*
> *her arm was another little baby in a pink blanket.*
>
> *He said, "See there, son, twin sisters! Now*
> *aren't you glad you prayed?"*
>
> *And the little boy said, "I sure am Dad, and*
> *aren't you glad I quit?"*

You can see what a light touch this is. It also announces to the audience that the speaker has finished. Mick uses it to say that this is the end of his speech.

There are many other examples, but be sure you don't end a speech with a humorous story after you have delivered a somewhat serious message. They simply do not go hand in hand and you leave the audience somewhat confused.

Getting Off

There are two schools of thought on the subject of thanking an audience at the finish of your speech. There are those who say that the audience is the one to do the thanking and they do it with their applause; they would say the speaker has prepared carefully to bring them a message and he or she deserves their thanks.

There is another group of speakers who say they would never end a speech without thanking their audience for being a good audience and for listening. Both of these ideas have merit.

I particularly like the way the late Bill Alexander, who

was a nationally known minister and fine public speaker from Oklahoma City, ended his speeches. He got through with his speech and down to what he had chosen as his closing remarks. These would be anywhere from one to three minutes of additional material. When he came to this transition point, he looked at his audience and said, "I want to thank you for having me here today and for your kind attention; you've been a wonderful audience." Then he would go into his close, and when he ended with the passage meant for closing, he would sit down. In this way he accomplished both things. He thanked the program people for having him and the audience for being a good audience, and yet he gave them the opportunity to show their thanks and appreciation by whatever applause and ovation they chose to give him. I use this method of ending a speech more than any other.

Regardless of how you feel about it, it is not something to belabor. You simply say "thank you." There is no need to start another message. "Thank you for being a wonderful audience," or "thank you for being here today," is sufficient, and then sit down. Either one is correct. It is simply a matter of taste and choice, as you see it. Learn to close with class. Whichever style you choose, make it smooth and capitalize on the feeling you have developed within the audience, so your close will have impact. Many speeches are ruined by a poor close. If you want to get your audience to remember you, and more importantly, if you want them to do what you ask, work on your closing techniques to be sure that you are taking advantage of your last opportunity to practice the *power of audience control.*

*****

As Cavett Robert says: "School is never out for the pro. . . ."

16

Professional Tips on Getting Better as a Speaker

It's up to you . . .

Other Speakers

The best method for improving your speech making is to hear as many other speakers as possible live. You can do this to some extent as you appear on various programs. Get down to the meeting room to listen to other speakers. Take the time frequently to stay after you speak, if others are to follow. See and hear their programs. You can study the audience reaction as the other speakers deliver. Analyzing an audience is a continuing source of learning and it pays large dividends. You can analyze not only what the speaker says, but also the gestures and body language used to breathe life into the speech as it is delivered. This way, you actually learn from the poor, the mediocre, and the effective speakers. You learn what *to* do as well as what *not* to do.

Tape

Today's speaker has many opportunities for self-improvement with the use of cassette tapes. Tape recorders and cassette recorders for taping are used by almost every speaker for self-improvement. You can put the cassette recorder on the podium or near the front of the room to record as your speech is delivered. You could have a friend tape it for you. Some convention programs do their own taping and will make them available to you. The important thing is to learn from these tapes after you get them.

You can play them over and over. Each time you will recognize the good parts of your talk and you can learn what passages were best received. This is especially true of the humorous passages. You can also tell by the quietness of your audience how well they were listening to your more serious passages. The important thing is to get and study the tapes, so you can improve in the areas in which you are weak. Your timing can be improved as you concentrate on your tempo and your change of pace.

Another method where taping is extremely helpful is in preparing a new speech. The use of new material as part of a speech, or rehearsing for an especially important speech, can be done on tape, analyzed, and improved greatly. These are important factors in helping you become a better, more effective speaker. You can then do exactly what has been asked of you when you were invited to speak. Make use of this marvelous tool and if you do not have one, get one.

You can also buy good recorded speeches of other speakers that you can study for their timing and their delivery, but do not try to copy them. If your conscience allows, steal some stories and other material. It is being done by many, and in most cases you do not have to worry about "borrowing" a story from another speaker.

Self-Analysis

Do not be too rough on yourself, but by all means, be self-critical. Work on all areas where you feel that you could do better. You replay tapes for just one purpose, to get better. There is no need to replay the recorded speeches if you are not going to learn to improve. It is your improvement that makes it such a valuable aid.

Listen for the flaws. Most every speech has some high points and some rather weak points. Listen for those carefully as you play back the recorded speeches. No one will have to point them out to you.

There may be words you are not pronouncing clearly. You may be talking too fast or too slow, or in an attempt to change pace, you may almost shout into the microphone. Study these things so that you can get these flaws out and give your speech with style and finesse. I am not suggesting that you try to be a perfect speaker, but I am suggesting that you make solid improvements constantly.

Vary Your Message

Once you have prepared your message well, and you can support a point with various anecdotes and humorous passages, learn to use all of them, though not all in one speech. As you give a speech over and over, as most popular speakers do, learn to use different material. It will help you and keep you from being bored with your own speech. It also presents a challenge.

The actor has to play the same role night after night and gets tired of delivering those lines, but since that is the way the play is written, the actor does not have the license to change the lines. The speaker can change parts of a talk from time to time, presenting a challenge to give it a fresh sound to him or her. In this way, it is more sparkling and there will be a better delivery. So be sure to change your material occasionally, just so long as it relates.

Dr. Tom Hagaii, CPAE, the famous inspirational speaker from High Point, N.C., prides himself on being called back time and time again to address the same organization. He fills these return speaking engagements with only a short period of time from his last appearance on their program. All of his speeches are practically new for each occasion and that is why his speeches are always sparkling and fresh.

Dr. Hagaii's reputation for great material is well known to other professional speakers, and he is respected by all, not only for his fresh material, but for his sparkling delivery.

Speak as Often as Possible

In all the books and courses dealing with public speaking, speaking as often as possible is not emphasized enough. Speaking as often as possible is a sure way to grow and become more effective as a speaker. But if it is obvious you have bad speaking habits and you do nothing to improve them, time and experience and the number of speeches won't help.

I know, for example, an industrial executive , who to my knowledge has spoken hundreds of times over the period of the last 15 years. For some reason, he hasn't seemed to get any better. He still does not have a sparkling delivery. He still bores the audience with a monotone. Apparently he has made no effort to improve his ability to deliver a speech so that the audience will be excited and moved by what he has to say.

Speak as often as you possibly can, searching constantly for new material, new anecdotes, and humorous lines to use. There is no way that you can fail to improve, if you really want to, if you want to become better as a speaker. Of course, first, you must really want to. Take your message seriously, take your audience seriously, but whatever you do, never take yourself too seriously. More speakers fail, for more than any other reason, because they take themselves too seriously. When you become good as a speaker, you will be only one of many. If you allow yourself to feel that you are someone special because you are asked to speak, you are in for a humiliating experience. The audience recognizes attitude and will react accordingly. This may be the most important aspect of how to get control of the audience.

* * * * *

And now, ladies and gentlemen . . . I'm on!

Index

Other recommended books . . .

THE TOASTMASTER'S TREASURE CHEST

5,000 INDEXED ITEMS

H. V. Prochnow & H. V. Prochnow Jr. For toastmasters, businessmen, politicians — anyone likely to be called on for brief remarks — here is a storehouse of wit, wisdom, jokes, toasts, stories and quotations! An indispensable book for those involved in discussions, conferences, seminars, Rotary clubs, church groups, trade organizations. Provides you with well-prepared, stimulating, 'impromptu' remarks! *None of this duplicates the material in the Prochnow's companion volume.* **The Public Speaker's Treasure Chest** (over 500,000 copies sold).

PUBLIC SPEAKER'S TREASURE CHEST

H. V. Prochnow. Material never before available except by searching through a library of basic books and anthologies. Over 1,000 jokes, 500 witticisms and epigrams, 200 amusing definitions, 300 similes, 1,000 quotations, 100 colourful phrases, 350 proverbs — in fact, everything you need to make speeches and conversation in its field for speakers, toast-masters, and the large number of readers who simply want to improve their conversation.